# Earth Witch

*Finding Magic in the Land*

## BRITTON BOYD

Hier⊕phantpublishing

Cover design by Kathryn Sky-Peck
Print book interior design by Frame25 Productions

Hierophant Publishing
San Antonio, TX
www.hierophantpublishing.com

If you are unable to order this book from your local bookseller,
you may order directly from the publisher.

Library of Congress Control Number: 2022910056
ISBN 978-1-950253-31-9
10 9 8 7 6 5 4 3 2 1

# Contents

*To you, Holy Mother, who gives us all life.*

# Introduction

The land and witchcraft have always been intimately intertwined. Magic lives in the soil, in the backwoods, in the bones of the dead, and in seemingly desolate places in nature. It lives in spring blossoms, in summer fruits, and in fall harvests. At its core, it enables us to merge with these seasons and cycles and be in recognition of the landscapes in which we find ourselves. And, in the process, it leads us to a greater understanding of our own cycles and needs.

Like the earth itself, we often need a wintering of the soul in order to truly appreciate these landscapes. My goal in this book is to invite you to plunge your hands into the soil, to collect those bones, and to discover these seemingly desolate places where magic lives. I hope to help you find a pathway and lineage of witchcraft that is oriented toward a deeper personal connection to the land. My intention here is to encourage you to seek out that deep, mysterious connection with the earth, because this connection is so crucial to the practice of being a witch.

If you're new to witchcraft, this book can provide you a supple foundation of practices with which to work—ones that flex and bend with you as you spiral toward a yet unknown destination. If you're a seasoned witch, this book may either challenge or affirm your beliefs. In either case, this book is meant to have a little bite, to leave some grit between your teeth. It is my hope that this grit will strengthen your spiritual immune system and shift your personal microbiome.

The magic of the earth witch stands as anathema to capitalistic *haute couture* witchcraft. The tools and goods of the earth witch are found in thrift stores, and in boxes of free items found on the side of the road. They are traded and bartered. A sun-bleached shirt that is imbued with memories. An item that is lost and found again. The path of the earth witch is cyclical, weaving, and spiraling. It ebbs and flows, waxes and wanes. It is not a linear path of upward growth. It may, in fact, cause you to take two steps backward in order to take one step forward.

As I write this, I am witnessing the tail end of winter here in the high desert I call home. I feel myself stirring from a deep cycle of spiritual and physical hibernation. A restlessness grows inside of me to find the first blooms of the sagebrush steppe, yet they won't be here for a little while longer. While I grow restless inside, the land tells me to wait, to sleep, to dream, to be still and present to the existing moment. To move slowly in a continuous embrace of the darkness within and without.

As capitalism has crept insidiously into modern witchcraft and other spiritual traditions, witches have often felt this same restlessness as a need to advance their craft swiftly, to put it on public display, to rush forth in pursuit of what could be called spiritual materialism. Yet what we truly seek is a form of progress that cannot be measured in terms of dollars or possessions. It is only with time and an erotic merging of the land and ourselves over many seasons that we can experience something real and profound. I encourage you to give yourself the time and space to rest, digest, and think metaphorically.

## Walking the Earth

In 2017, I took an exceptionally long walk—2,660 miles to be exact. I walked from the Mexican border all the way to Canada following the Pacific Crest Trail. Over the course of six months, I trod through creeks raging from high snow melt, destructive wildfires, scorching deserts, and snowy mountain passes. This journey was one of the hardest and most gratifying things I have ever done.

When I started my hike on the Mexican border, I was brimming with excitement. I passed through the beautiful southwestern desert, taking shade beside massive boulders and collecting cool water that poured from rocks, from sources unknown. But when I made my first camp that night, the gravity of what I'd undertaken finally hit me. I felt lost and confused, and wondered what the hell I had gotten myself into. A sense of regret and a strange sadness descended upon me. I knew that what was about to transpire over the next several months would utterly change me, inside and out. I questioned whether I was even capable of it. When I awoke the next morning, I realized I had bedded down in a pile of decaying poison oak leaves. I itched horribly for days to come.

My journey through the desert broke me apart into millions of pieces. I endured a wrenching breakup with my partner and felt devastated and even more lost than before. I didn't sleep well for weeks, lost my appetite, and became an unholy burden to those around me. I cried all the time. I drifted off amid frogs, toads, scorpions, and tarantulas as I wept myself to sleep.

Then, during one particularly difficult afternoon, I just let everything go. I rolled a cigarette, knowing that smoking can be a prayer if you do it mindfully. As I took my final drag, I realized that life as I knew it was over. I had been fighting to keep everything the same, even though I knew that everything was changing. Right then, I committed to myself that I would stop looking backward. The path forward was the way for me. And it was this commitment to accepting change that helped me find a new path and add a whole new page to the book of life that I was writing.

For the rest of my hike, I gave myself up to the wonder of the land around me—the incredible elevations of the High Sierras, the devastatingly beautiful snow-melted raging creeks, the slippery icy passes, the flat, sometimes boring, stretches of high plains. The lush, dense forests of the Pacific Northwest provided a striking metaphor for just how easy it was to become disoriented and lose my bearings along the way. I endured the hot dry deserts of Oregon, snow squalls in mountain passes, bone-chilling cold, and raging wildfires along the Columbia River. The last 500 miles of my trek took nearly everything I had within me. But I was determined that nothing would keep me from moving forward.

Then, while walking through a massive old-growth forest one day, I felt the earth speak to me. I moved my consciousness into my heart center and listened to what the forest had to say while I walked. The trees were alert to the wildfire and the smell of smoke in the air. But they'd been there before a million times over—these ancient trees. They asked me to be present more often—or rather, showed me how—and requested that I not dwell on the bitterness of my past. It was a simple message really, but a transformative one when put into practice.

At that moment of understanding, I called upon my ancestors and spirits known to me, and I made another commitment. I pledged to orient my life to be in service to the earth and to them. I prayed for the right resources to help this to occur. I committed to making my new life different from my previous one—a life that facilitated a deeper connection to my work, to witchcraft, and to this deep calling to walk a spiritual path. I pledged to make this calling my life. Not something I engaged in on weekends, not something I practiced when the moon and stars were perfectly aligned, but every day. I would breathe it in, would work it and express it. I made an oath there and then that I would not stop, that I would persist to the end.

I carried a small handful of osha seeds with me that I'd gathered from a plant I greatly admired. This plant, known as bear root, resists conventional cultivation and loathes a civilized garden bed. Its seeds need the soil of mountains and snow melt to germinate. I had gathered a few handfuls of the seeds as a talisman of sorts so I could carry their magic with me. On this particular day, I scattered them to the wind, saying: "As you grow, so do I." I spoke aloud. While osha plants grow slowly, they grow more robust with age. I wanted to be like them. To resist conventional cultivation, to remain wild, and to flow with the ebbs and tides of the seasons. I knew that I *needed* these forces in my development.

The last days of my incredible 2,660-mile trek were particularly grueling, plagued by a raging whiteout blizzard. When I finally arrived at the end of my journey, I felt the rush of safety and security that a well-worn path provides. I was proud that I had met the challenge. But then I asked myself: "Now what?" Now, I had to fulfill the commitment I'd made to my spirits, to my ancestors, and to myself. That was my *now what:* To see my journey through to the end of the new path that had opened before me in the old-growth forest. My journey had given me new metaphorical tools to use along that path—going with the flow, not resisting when I faced roadblocks but, like the power of water, flowing freely and finding new ways around them, persisting through pain, and knowing when to rest. I didn't know where the path would lead, but I knew my next steps: Get home. Clean up. Find a new place to live. Start a new life.

On the way home, I found a lovely little yurt on some shared land in Oregon. The yurt provided me a place to "come down" from my hiking high, as well as a supportive community with whom to connect and share meals. It felt like home, and I sensed a strange peace there. So I set up my altars and arranged my few humble tools. Then I walked into the oak forest that surrounded my yurt. That forested refuge became my protective cauldron-like space in which to process everything and open new doors.

## Finding the Path

So, what does this long-distance hike have to do with being an earth witch? Lots of things, but let's focus on two of them for now.

First, this hike reminded me of something that I already knew deep in my bones. It reminded me that, throughout the ages, witchcraft has naturally been earth-based, as it uses the plants, roots, and stones that are available within a local ecology. In this sense, the phrase "earth witch" is similar to the phrase "wet water." The truth is that the practice of witchcraft has always been tied to the earth, and my hope is that by the end of this book you will understand that all you need for your practice is right beneath your feet. You don't have to purchase anything.

Second, we often mistakenly assume that our practice will follow a straight and narrow path—free from obstruction, free from getting lost, free from injury, free from pain, free from consequences. But just like my 2,660-mile trek, the path of an earth witch defines neither a linear nor a static journey. Like nature, this path ebbs and flows; it breathes and pulses. So, how do we maintain the tenacity required to persevere along our path through the ups and downs of life?

It takes both incredible will and incredible surrender, and knowing which one you need at a particular time is part of the art of witchcraft. Unfortunately, you will not always be on a spiritual high when walking the path of the earth witch. It will be beautiful for sure. However, you will also have your down moments when you wonder just what the hell you've gotten yourself into. Sometimes, it will seem as if you've veered far off the path, becoming lost and confused. But that's part of the journey, too. I wandered off the main path of my long hike many times, but I always made it back, in part because I always knew when I'd lost the trail. The tracks before me looked different, and I felt a strange sense that something was "off." The same is true of life. We have a cord of connection to our primary path and, when we veer away from it, it pulls us back. It lets us know we've gone off-track.

Moreover, there is value in veering off the path. So many that I meet ask: "Am I on the right path? How do I know I am on the path I want to be on?" No matter where you are, you're on the right path. Not being on your "true" path is a part of the journey—you'll always find your way back. Little jaunts off the main trail are an adventure. They help us see what we might not have seen otherwise. We may find treasure, like a particularly good patch of huckleberries, a stunning view, or a very old tree to gaze upon in wonder. Going off-track teaches us how to get back on that well-worn path that brings us surety and the inner knowing that we're on the correct trajectory. So, fear not if you feel that you're not quite on the path you want to be on. You're on an adventure—a quest—and you'll be pulled back to your own unique equilibrium in due time.

## How to Use This Book

Witchcraft isn't a phase; it isn't a fashionable moment we have in the height of its cultural popularity. It is a way of being and a way of life. Maybe it works for you; maybe it doesn't. But if you choose this path and commit to it, life will be full, beautiful, and challenging.

Walking this path is an ongoing practice, even when the light dims or when you feel blinded by it.

To that aim, I offer this book as one small guide to return your withcraft to the energy of the land and all that this includes. As you will see in the pages that follow, this entails more than what you may initially think, like nature, plants, and animals. It is also your body, which is of the earth. It is also your spirit, which is connected to your body and therefore also of the earth. It is also your ancestors, who were of the earth, and your dreams, which are how the earth may be speaking to you. As you will see, all these things are connected, because we are all one and all equal.

You'll also notice in these pages that I do not refer to spirits or plants as "it" but as "they," "them," and "who." This clarifying distinction is very important to me, as it gives animacy to what is considered inert and dead matter in modern culture. Plants and spirit are living and breathing beings, and I refer to them as such here. And I use the word "spirit" to refer to the animate intelligence that lives all around us.

Furthermore, I want to be clear that it's not enough just to read and think about the ideas I share here. You must do the work and bring them into your practice. For this reason, I include specific practices at the end of each chapter that I have found integral to making a conscious connection to the earth and all that surrounds us. You'll find a list of these practices in the Appendix at the end of the book. The practices outlined here can help you become a witch who listens to the voice of the land and the earth. I call these "practices" to remind you that they are ongoing and never perfect.

While I feel that you can perform these practices anywhere—no matter where you are geographically—it's impossible for me not to be influenced in my own practice by my own surroundings of the high desert in eastern Oregon, and you will see this clearly in the book. What I encourage you to do is to rely in a similar way on your own unique surroundings. (You likely already are.) For we are all intimately influenced by our environment, whether we know it or not. If you feel lost or disconnected, simply keep reading. My intent is to help you see the sacredness right beneath your feet, right outside your door.

While a long-distance hike like mine is done in a season—spring or summer—the spiritual practice of witchcraft is both year-round and lifelong. Seeing it in this way may seem daunting, as there will be times in your craft when you may not feel like practicing. These are normal phases. Knowing when to push yourself and when to rest is key. You will find your own path-walking rhythm. Small steps, they say; don't walk too fast; just move at a comfortable yet persistent pace. One person I hiked with was affectionately called Little Engine. She walked slowly, but always made it. We each have our own pace. Some are jackrabbits who speed and stop, while others are like tortoises, slow and persistent. Find your own special rhythm and don't compare it to another's. You move at your pace because that is what works for you.

Your enthusiasm will wax and wane just like the moon, so remember this: When you lose the trail, lapse, or take a long break, getting back into the flow of things can be a painful and sometimes disorienting process. Learning how to get back on track is a valuable exercise and the more you do it, the better you'll get at sharpening those tools that help you return to the path. If you fall off the metaphorical wagon, fear not. You can always pick up the trail where you left off. It's not going anywhere. It's there, waiting for you.

Now, let us begin.

# Chapter 1

# Heeding the Call

*We are born with whirlwinds, forest fires, and comets inside us.
We are born able to sing to birds and read the clouds and see our
destiny in grains of sand. But then we get the magic educated
right out of our souls. We get it churched out, spanked out,
washed out, and combed out. We get put on the straight and
narrow and told to be responsible. Told to act our age. Told to
grow up, for God's sake. And you know why we were told that?
Because the people doing the telling were afraid of our wildness
and youth, and because the magic we knew made them ashamed
and sad of what they'd allowed to wither in themselves.*
—Robert R. McCammon

To feel the call to witchcraft is to feel the call of the
wild. It is to be lured into otherness—to be different.
Sometimes we feel it in our breath. The wind whispering of mystery, sweeping away dust motes and uncovering what was hidden, but there all along. Sometimes
it appears in the quickening of our blood, like spring
sap rising as we root deeper into the soil. It's a pulse

that reverberates something subtle, but with a rumble of distant thunder, bringing awareness of the deepest caverns of our hearts. It can move and bend like a river, molecules reshaping and changing with every ripple and rapid. It can move us from the trance of ordinary life and into a strange otherworldly wakefulness. Sometimes it can feel like a crackling fire, all-consuming and radically transforming. It can feel devastatingly beautiful. It is at this crossroads that the realm of earth witchery truly unfolds for us.

The call to earth witchery can arrive in various ways, and it will be as unique for you as your fingerprints. Sometimes you stumble into it haphazardly and stub your toe on the way through the door. You don't have to experience a brilliant white-light moment to wake up to what's inside of you. Sometimes it's simply a quiet knowing. It's following the stars that are all scattered in the dirt beneath your feet. You move on paws and claws, fingering your way through the soil, letting whiskers and eyes well-adjusted to the mysteries of the night guide you.

The point is: You feel it. You know it, and you can identify it moving through your blood. Our modern culture typically suggests one of two things: at best, it urges you to shrug off this feeling as a simple daydream; at worst, it encourages you to call it a sinful urge that must be avoided at all costs. What should you do with this sensation? Above all, don't ignore it, don't disbelieve it, and don't be afraid of it. Don't let anyone tell you what it is and is not. There are forces greater than yourself that are ready to guide you and move you to the path on which you're meant to walk. The land summons its lost children, bringing us home and into the arms of belonging.

My own call to witchcraft came in a rather inelegant way. I knew something was *up*, that something had shifted within me. I was at a crisis point and seeking power and agency when I felt I had none. I sensed a desperation and knew I was in need of something more. I was in a terrifying, abusive relationship that I felt I could not escape, freshly unemployed, and stressing about the future. While watching a documentary on the Salem witch trials to numb myself out, something powerful awoke within me. It was as if I remembered something that I'd forgotten, but I didn't quite know what it was. I knew that it was a very old and familiar memory, but I could not place it. From that moment on, nothing would ever be the same again.

A strange whisper kept calling me, but I did not know which path to take. My walks to and from the corner stores suddenly came alive—everything was animate and dynamic. Small mossy worlds with multitudes of lichen life, dandelions reaching for the sun from the cracks in pavement, crows speaking their curious language from the tops of fruit trees. What I had so often seen as inert dead mass was suddenly more alive to me and I was now privy to it.

Around that time, wildly synchronistic events began playing out in my dreams. In one dream, I followed a slight and nearly invisible trail. I picked up feathers, strange rocks, and small keys, and listened to bird song in the canopy of the local forested park. I heard a voice speaking, though it didn't speak to me in English. I noticed a faint pathway through the weeds and noisy streets, and passed a squirrel chittering on my neighbor's fence just outside my bedroom window. I was observing more, and I was letting that and my curiosity lead me. A light was growing inside me that would soon become a lantern to illuminate a starlit path.

As this path opened before me, I simply followed the signs. I knew that if I did not, I would die miserable and always wonder what could have been. I refused to make that my legacy. Instead, I wanted to know that I had lived life to its fullest and to the best of my ability.

It takes great courage to walk the crooked path through the forest, desert, hills, and mountains. But whatever landscape you encounter, it will guide you. You just must trust in it and take that first step. You may wring your hands over your experiences and calling, but do something with them. Take action. You belong here and are worthy of them. I can't tell you what your next step is, but you will know it in your heart. Let it guide your way.

## What's In a Name?

Society is fascinated by witches and can sense their otherness. But true witchcraft is being co-opted and transformed by our capitalist culture every day. We see this in the instant witch kits that are sold online and at big chain stores. We see it in the carefully arranged presentations on social media that imply that witchcraft is only ever something that is comely and attractive. Certainly, witchcraft can be beautiful, but these portrayals are just "white picket fence" versions of the Craft that keep its wild nature hidden. While some strains and currents of witchcraft are defying this oppressive cultural influence, others are eager to accept it and submit to it.

Witches are often portrayed as those who are shunned, or as outcasts or scapegoats. The image of a queer person who lives on the edge of the wood is found throughout mythology and folklore. And it is in this imagery and archetype that we can find one of the many root tendrils of witchcraft.

The historical record shows that those who were accused of witchcraft often met spirits at a moment of crisis in their lives—when a husband or child fell ill, when a crop failed, when cows were sick and not lactating. It was in these moments, when they themselves were pushed to their physical limits or left to manage difficult situations on their own, that an opening appeared for spirit contact. These moments of distress and spiritual crises are what enable us to connect more deeply with a powerful source outside of ourselves. It is important that we understand this historical context because, very often, such an awakening is preceeded by an agonizing ordeal. At these moments, we often stand at a crossroads—the liminal point where choices are made that change the direction of our lives.

The word "witch" has always evaded strict definition. But one thing is certain: The word arouses suspicion and carries weight, even in this day and age when being a witch is considered in vogue. But when you call yourself a witch, you're actually opening a portal. You're sending out a calling card to the realm of the unseen that you're ready to do the work. And let me assure you: It takes *work* to be a witch and the spirits will hold you to your word. To be a witch is to hold beauty in one hand and terror in the other. It is dangerous work and not for the faint of heart.

You do not have to call yourself a witch to be one, but there is deep meaning in taking on the title if you choose to do so. While anyone can call themselves a witch, the question is: What does it *really* take to be a witch? While it may be upsetting for some to read, not everyone has what it takes to practice witchcraft.

To claim the title of witch requires that you understand all those who came before you. We all stand upon the shoulders, backs, and bones of our witch ancestors. This lineage that we join is an important part of who we become. When you take on the title of witch, you claim the spiritual heritage of all those who were burned, hanged, drowned, and more for who they were, and of those who still continue to suffer under oppression—our human and non-human kin, and the land. We orient our actions toward them and give them our allegiance. While those who came before you may not be related by blood, you are definitely related to them in a web of interdependence. They will, indeed, inform your practice, and this is a great responsibility to carry.

Witches are naturally rebellious and always stand in opposition to the status quo. They perpetually disrupt institutions that seek to bring them under their heel. Witches always speak for those without a voice—the unseen, the discarded, and the oppressed. They are rebels with a cause, with a proclivity for spirit contact and for speaking for those who've been pushed into silence. We each have our own unique gifts and talents. Your witchcraft will not look like that of others.

As I mentioned in the Introduction, of this we can be sure: Witchcraft orients itself by the voice of the land, by the earth beneath our feet, and by our non-human kin. Witchcraft works with the web of life, and we are a part of that web. It is the means through which we connect with the earth and make contact with the spirits. It is the channel through which wisdom and understanding come to aid others. It is the lens through which we see the self-evolving and changing nature of the world as time passes.

The intentions of a witch are often marked by passion and an innocence of heart. Witches desire to know more—to *do* more. It is in the doing that the actions we take not only inform our craft, but create it.

## Capitalism and the Land

In today's world, witchcraft is often viewed as a tool for self-empowerment by those who feel disenfranchised by modern culture. A call to the Craft often originates in need and desperation when we are in tight spots, or when we are undergoing a radical reawakening in our spiritual lives that is brought about by the challenges we face. It is here that we're given an opportunity to connect to something greater than ourselves. Witchcraft is not merely a simple tool for self-empowerment or self-help, however. To think that it is is short-sighted and, dare I say, problematic and potentially dangerous. The pendulum of witchcraft has swung too far in the direction of our modern self-help culture and needs to swing back to its true purpose—acting in service to the earth and the land we inhabit.

Pop-culture witchcraft is marked by a narcissism that needs to be reevaluated. Narcissism + spell work = modern capitalistic witchcraft. And this is a trend I seek to disrupt with this book. Our radical self-love and self-improvement culture has tipped so far off center that we no longer recognize the texture of the living earth beneath our feet. In popular witchcraft, we selfishly extract what we need and rarely give back. And this is where capitalism has stealthily crept in. This selfish inward gaze cannot see outside itself. The land and spirits themselves call—no, beg—for a shift and reorientation in our vision.

Dams that destroy the lives of already endangered salmon and domesticate rivers that once ran wild, industries that raze the last stands of old-growth forest, mines that extract the limited supply of rare minerals for our electric cars, biological warfare on our plant kin, a sea of endless monocrops that choke out diversity, wind farms that create a deadly vacuum for insect and bird life, pipelines routed through sacred indigenous lands destroying water sources, acidified oceans—this is but a mere fraction of what civilization has wrought upon on the earth. Our eyes and hearts are so conditioned to accept this as the status quo. But I implore you to realize that we do, indeed, have the ability to lift the veil that has shrouded our eyes. And a well-oriented witch knows how to do just this.

If we are to recover from the scourge of capitalism, we must surrender our will to a higher power—just like addicts recovering from their addictions. This can be a deity, the earth itself, a mountain, a river, a spirit of place—whoever calls to you. It is through this portal that you can find a way to be in service to the land and give back. It is an emptying of the self so that a greater power may move into you and guide you.

If we're going to save the earth and non-human life, if we're going to be accomplices in the work of subverting the destructive powers that be, we must act in service to the land and its inhabitants. This action requires that we decentralize human control and look beyond the narrow scope of self-gratification that modern witchcraft has adopted. This isn't to say that you should do work that deprives you of material things. We all have a right to what we need to survive and have some level of comfort in our lives. However, you can still be a part of this work by committing to be in service to something greater than yourself.

To do this work effectively, you must have an ear to the ground listening to the spirit. It's why I speak of finding a higher power—God or a spirit of your understanding—to work with and to fulfill you so that you recognize where and how to carry out this work. They will help you find your orientation.

Gathering the material goods for your practice—crystals, cards, tools, and the like—will not make you a witch. Aesthetics can be important to your identity, but they do not make you a witch. Your actions do that. In fact, I challenge you as you read this book to buy no tools for your practice. Chances are, you already have everything you need anyway. What are fancy knives for, if not to cut the cords that bind us to dominant structures that seek to destroy and consume all life on our blessed planet? Grab a knife that works for you and cut the cord.

So consider: Are you amassing trinkets, or are you listening deeply to the land and to spirit? (We will delve more into deep listening later in the book.)

As you begin the work of opening yourself, or recognizing the opening, you must come to understand your character flaws. You must get to know yourself and be understanding of your passions and where they can lead you. Passion is a powerful driving force. But left unchecked, it can become a disorienting and destructive element within you. Rigorous honesty about who you are, what you have done, where you originated, and the issues with which you must contend within yourself can inform your process and keep you grounded. As the incredible author and poet Nayirah Waheed wrote: "The greatest teacher will send you back to yourself."

## Validating Your Craft

I spent many years seeking validation through teachers and guides, resulting in a plague of hopelessness. With a deep longing and sadness, I sought a sense of belonging, but I could not find it in the usual places. I found it in the aftermath of lovers who broke my heart, and in teachers I discovered were corrupt and who took me in only to turn me away. I've always felt that I was grasping at smoke and that my only way of being a witch was to become "certified" by another. But I know now there are other ways.

What my teachers did teach me may not seem like a mystery of the Craft, but it was important nonetheless. They taught me to be discerning in my studies. They taught me how to follow the red thread—the tendrils of witchcraft that run through the tapestry of life—and the current of the Craft through my reading. Witches spend much of their time with their noses stuck in books—just as you are doing now as you read. My teachers taught me how to extract information in a way that could help me understand the history and context of the Craft. For the time that I spent in their beautiful sun-dappled living room discussing books and how to make tea, I am very thankful.

Many students of witchcraft come to teachers with high expectations that they will come away with whatever they seek. The truth is that, as students, we should graciously take what we receive. I was given the gift of understanding how to study texts of the Craft properly, which proved invaluable to me. I learned the importance of highlighting texts and taking notes. I learned the importance of openness and curiosity, and of approaching everything with a beginner's mind. These are valuable lessons that I have carried through life.

For me and my path, I found further teachings and initiation through the plants, the land, my ancestors, and in unusual spaces. On a beach collecting stones, letting river water slip and swirl through my fingers, touching boulders, and sheltering in the behemoth shadow of mountains. Sometimes, things look very different from what we expect or daydream.

In our modern culture, we don't honor the wisdom of elders. Our society is obsessed with the cult of youth, and we deeply fear aging and death. The true apprenticeship model is extremely rare today, possibly even dead. For many of us, our elders are lost or dying, and teachers within traditions are increasingly hard to find or are inaccessible to us because of distance or circumstances. If you do find the opportunity to be in relationship to an elder, treasure it and offer them your time selflessly and without an expectation of gain. You can learn much within these relationships. Having a teacher will not validate or invalidate your personal practice, however. The action of practice validates your witchcraft and your connection to the land on which you live.

It is important to understand that, when we seek teachers, we are seeking them to transform our own darkness and pain into something that will make us more powerful. The irony is that, when we seek out teachers, we are really looking for ourselves through them. Time and time again, I have seen folks hand over their power in the hopes that a teacher or guide will take their soul to the proverbial crucible and reforge them into something shiny and new—a powerful version that the student may then conveniently take back.

If only it were that easy.

Such thinking can potentially lead to deep disappointment and disillusionment on your path. The work of becoming is an internal process, which is sometimes facilitated by an outside source. But always, that transformation happens from within.

It is wise to approach teachers with a recognition of their humanity. They also make bad decisions and have their own shadows with which to contend. Part of the reason we seek them out is to observe that they have done their own work of shedding their skin and being reborn. We note their power and how they wield it. We believe that they can be examples who inspire us to seek the way back to our own power, personal agency, and understanding of the self.

While you may have many guides and teachers on your path, they likely will not show up exactly as you expect them to. A good teacher doesn't need to identify as a proper witch. It is by noticing themes and their orientation with the land and spirit that you will build your discernment. Many teachers may not even come in human form. Very often, they are spirits, or a presence that is embedded in the land, or lights that shine down on you as moon and starlight. It is in opening yourself to the inherent wisdom of the land you inhabit and honoring it that you find your greatest teacher—or a multitude of them.

Teachers can show up as pain, as weeds growing in the cracks of a street, as an elderly woman you meet on a bus, as trauma, as a weathered old tree, as an ecstatic union with a lover, as illness, as the heart of a mountain, as art, as death, as a flower, as loss, as an ancestor, as a broken heart, as a particularly peculiar rock, or even as a beloved book, as well as in many other strange and curious places. Know then, that your greatest teachers can be non-human. Seek them out, for they are right outside your door. Whole worlds and other intelligences exist that desire to share and give their knowledge. Rocks, trees, plants, mountains, rivers, and other features of the land have much knowledge to share. If you feel that human intercession is required on your path, pray that your crooked journey leads you to a wise and gracious teacher who can show you the way. Remember, however, that this is not required. A witch can find a teacher in all things—this is our gift and our birthright.

## Initiation of an Earth Witch

It is important to speak about initiation, especially within the context of teachers and covens. Some feel that they must be initiated into a particular tradition or coven to become witches. While coven and tradition initiation have their merits, I feel the notion of initiation as a goal in itself is false. If you're reading this book and resonating with the text, I will hazard a guess that you were born a witch and that it is naturally already a part of you. The very act of doing the work that follows is initiation in and of itself. You have already begun your initiation by picking up this book. You will, in fact, be initiated many times throughout your life and undergo many layers of initiation.

Spirit will initiate you. You're initiated the moment you traverse the path that is unfolding before you now. This isn't to say that initiation within a tradition isn't a powerful experience, because it is. But don't let it be a hang-up for you and don't let it stop you. Witches can be both born and made. How this unfolds for you is unique to you and your path. You will know what is right for you. Allow your process to be informed by spirit and by the land.

Witchcraft is non-dogmatic. It is wildness. Too often, I see gatekeepers denying and shaming people to keep them from awakening into and embracing this identity. If anyone tells you that you must pass through their initiation rite to become a witch, turn away. Times change and so does witchcraft. Witchcraft is not a static or linear practice. It ebbs and flows as the world's life blood does. Within this is a pulse, a reverberation of change that echoes through the land and calls us to action.

It is up to you whether you take on the title of "witch," or "earth witch," or no title at all. I knew early on in my path that I desperately wanted to merge with the identity of a witch, but I felt a lack of belonging and worthiness. If you find yourself at a similar crossroads, I hope this book will guide you into taking the steps that will provide you with the proof, through the actions that you take, that you are indeed worthy of this title. Many feel that titles mean nothing, or that that they do not carry weight. I argue that they do.

Calling yourself a witch is still a dangerous and radical act, however. Just tell others that you're a witch and watch their whole demeanor change. Being a witch can result in loneliness, ostracization, and more. Jobs have been lost and family connections destroyed. You needn't be public about your identity. But if you know in your heart that this is your identity, claim it!

*Practice: Signs You Are an Earth Witch*

If you are new to the path, the following list of signs may help you to know that you aren't alone in experiencing these feelings. And of course, these signs may look different for you. For many witches, the signs are woven into their dreams and the whisperings of plants. They may appear as the pierced stone you find in a riverbed that, when held up to your eye, lets you peer into another world—the Otherworld—that is interlaced with the living world that surrounds you.

Here are some signs that you may be awakening to this new path:

- You make things happen. When you envision or feel something, it somehow comes to be.

- When faced with challenges, you transmute them into power, wisdom, and understanding. You feel and acknowledge the pain of an experience, but you move through it and allow it to inform your process and your becoming. It feeds your soul, but it does not inhibit you.

- You have what may be considered an unusual connection to non-human kin, places, and objects. You simply know you are connected to them, and often you know more than others know themselves.

- You're magnetic; you often attract attention from humans and non-humans alike. You draw people in because of your connection to mystery and the forbidden. Sometimes this can create problems, because witches are often seen as the source of both trouble and solace. This paradox is maddeningly alluring.

- You have a rich interior life and vivid imagination. As a child, you may have been scolded for being a "daydreamer." Your rich inner life makes trance states, journeying, and hedge-riding (taking a spiritual journey into the Otherworld or the collective unconscious) easy.

- You have a brazen and powerful sexuality or eroticism. Strong sexual currents are strong magical currents. Knowing how to direct sexual energy is an act of witchcraft.

- You're often a heretic. You disrupt and defy the status quo of organized institutions and their ways of being.

- Accepting that you're a witch becomes a matter of life and death for you. Denying or avoiding your witchcraft becomes a serious problem for you. Often, this ordeal is the precursor to an awakening.

# Chapter 2

# A Time to Rewild

*Rewilding is not about abandoning civilization, but about enhancing it. It is to "love not man the less, but Nature more."*
—George Monbiot

The notion that all of us are somehow separate from nature or separate from the non-human world (i.e., spirit) is a construct of Western civilization and the dogma of institutionalized religion. This notion has continually sought to separate us from the natural world and to exploit it. One of its basic tenets is that man is meant to dominate the land, rather than live in harmony with it, and this has led us to collapsing ecologies and rapid climate change.

The notion that "wild" nature is "out there"—that witchcraft is "out beyond"—is a civilized construct that leaves us with a sense that we are separated from it and not already intimately connected to it. In our modern-day socio-political climate, "wilderness" is seen as land that is set aside and devoid of human connection, saved for recreation and pleasure. This has not always been the case, however. This land was tended by the indigenous peoples who originally inhabited it. Wilderness, as conceived of today, is a concept developed by a capitalist culture that views the land as a resource and values nature for what can be extracted from it—wood, animals, food, shelter, and so on.

This flawed view has created a dichotomy of "wild" versus "wilderness." Before European settlers landed in North America, the land was a veritable garden, tended with care and valued for thousands of years by indigenous folks. They are still here tending the land, and they fight tirelessly to protect it. It is important to understand this as we move forward with the process of unlearning what we have been taught and of connecting to the earth.

This dichotomy created a separation between us and the land, and this notion of separation is deeply ingrained in us all by modern culture. Indeed, our minds have built fences to keep out what is considered wild and unruly, and we continually seek to dominate and control nature's narrative. But witches see themselves as *merging with* what is beyond the hedge or border. Witches listen to the land. They understand it. They integrate with it.

The idea of fences, hedges, or borders between worlds can be helpful when we reach out to witchcraft and when those in that liminal world reach out to us. It is in these spaces in-between that life flourishes, where we can grab a handful of wild blackberries that nourish us. This is where we can "rewild" our spirits and bodies as we divest from capitalist culture, and ultimately from civilization.

For what we consume becomes the stuff of which we are made. If your days are spent with your eyes locked on a TV or a computer screen, the flashing images you see there will surely be reflected in your inner constitution. So when it comes to your daily practice, consider your priorities. What *really* matters to you? Staying updated on the infinite scroll of social media, or quieting your mind so you can hear and see the wild spirit moving within and around you? What is more important to you? It's up to you to decide.

Many years ago, when I was a young witch embarking upon my journey, I felt something was missing. I went through the motions of full moon and new moon rites and rituals, calling upon the old ones to guide me on my path. I spent many a night and early morning with incense swirling and hot coffee or tea in hand, praying to my ancestors and spirits. I picked my way along forested paths, collecting herbs and wild plants during different lunar phases and on the high and holy days of the equinoxes and solstices. I performed rites to honor the dead and the spirits. I lit candles to bring in prosperity and for healing when I was ailing. By all rights, I was practicing the old ways.

Yet something was absent from my life as a fledgling witch. The missing piece for me was a daily practice that reminded me of my place within the web of the earth and how to connect with this within my own life's rhythms. I sought a deeper connection. For, if I was to be a witch, it couldn't be something I just did occasionally during certain moon cycles. It had to be something *I am*. Much of what I had read or discovered placed emphasis on lunar rites and rituals and spell work, but I craved a deeper spiritual practice.

I realized that I needed to create inner spaces for my daily practice and weave them into the fabric of my life. I needed to merge with and walk the path between worlds, rather than living separate from it. My practice was right there before me, just as yours is, to grasp onto and breathe in. But I needed to create space for this pulse to expand within and around me, space in which my ancestors and the spirits could reach out to guide me. I had to meet them halfway, and I had to create the inner spaces in which this could happen.

As I considered my own struggle to establish a meaningful practice of witchcraft, I realized that what I really needed to do was to "rewild" myself—to reestablish an intimate connection to the wild world around me. Sometimes it takes drastic action to initiate changes in our lives that we know are in alignment with our calling. For me, it was my hike along the Pacific Crest Trail. After I finished this total-immersion experience in nature, I became allergic to cities. After hiking for months through mountainous landscapes, cities were too busy, too loud, and too bright for my rewilded body and mind. I found a yurt on the edge of a forest where I could process my experience. It was there that I began to prioritize my practice and realized that my spiritual needs came first and foremost.

I must be honest with you, however. It wasn't all dew-covered mosses and rainbows, although there was a lot of that. I took a major financial hit and lost a lot in the way of material possessions. But I gained more in the realm of the spiritual. All of us need money to survive in this world, but not at the cost of a deadened spirit, an endless longing, and a painful acknowledgment of what could have been.

You don't have to hike thousands of miles or live in a yurt in the woods to accomplish this shift, however. Maybe for you, rewilding looks like quitting your draining job for work that is more fulfilling, or relocating to your dream high-desert home in New Mexico. If you have an inkling of what your calling looks and feels like for you, reach for it.

Reaching for what we desire can often feel very dreamlike. We get wrapped up in the fantasy of what we desire and linger in dream states that don't lead us to action. We must ground our dreams in the soil for them to take root and this looks like practical and often boring work. I set a goal, drafted a timeline, set financial goals, and took every opportunity that moved me closer to my dream. When you orient every step in the direction of your dream, you can come to live it.

To establish my own connection to the wild world, I reevaluated where I spent my time. For example, I limited my use of screens and quit playing video games, both of which were really only a form of escapism from my unexciting and often depressed existence. But withdrawing from technology was a hardship I was willing to accept, and honestly a minor pain to endure in the grand scheme of things. I dissected my daily and weekly schedules and found where I could weave in my practice and open space for it. By releasing mere distractions, I was able to concentrate on my vision and give my practice ample room to flourish.

And every time I took a hiatus from social media and immersed myself in the natural world around me, I started creating art—something that brings me deep joy and satisfaction, something I never found in the mindless and endless surfing of the Internet. Getting back in touch with the wild world created an expansive space in which my internal landscape could grow and flourish. Give it a try to discover how much creative energy is freed up within you. Try it for a week or a month and see what happens to both your psyche and your habits.

If you do not prioritize your witchcraft over the distractions of society, you will never be able to reconnect to the wild world around you. If you continue to believe that the natural world—the wild world—is out of reach, it will remain that way. But if you reorient yourself to connect with spirit and the non-human world, you will reconnect with your own inner landscape. Chances are it's there waiting for you. Open your palm, turn it up toward the sun, the moon, and the stars, and let them in. Consider where you can reorient your time and how it is spent. If you're serious about your path and how it will unfold for you, you must make space for it to happen. You must orient yourself in the direction of the experience.

As this need to create inner space established itself within me, I noticed that my mornings were devoid of any rituals besides my necessary cup of coffee. I then began journaling to record my dreams and thoughts, and any experiences I had with spirit. I found that the pre-dawn hours held a special kind of liminal magic, where only the crepuscular creatures moved about, the stars still shown, and dawn gave way to a new day. It was the perfect time for me to set my daily intentions, so that I could embody and walk my path through each moment. These precious hours have become sacred to me, and I make sure that I am always present for them, even if it means waking up at 4:30 in the morning.

Establishing this shift has become the cornerstone of my practice. Thirteen years later, I am still waking up early, lighting candles, setting incense, and watching the dew descend upon the plants as I ready myself for a new day. When you start your day with spirit and dedication, it follows you through the rest of the day. It helps you know where you stand. When you become more present in the moment—when you create inner space and step into it—the spirit can fill and guide you, as it has for me.

Not everyone can wake up before dawn, however. Maybe your day begins at dusk or noon, when the sun is at its apex. The point is not *when* you create that sacred space; the point is that you *do* it. In the coming chapters, we'll explore how you can create this space and how you may want to fill it. For now, here are some simple ways you can connect with the wild world and create space in which your practice can grow and become a foundation for you.

## Minimize Distractions

Relinquishing activities that only serve to distract you from your soul's calling is a necessary and sacred act. When you do this, you signal that you're serious and willing to make the commitment. Take stock of where you find yourself drifting. Do you spend an inordinate amount of time on social media? Our modern existence is caught up in a bewildering muddle of information and imagery. Experiment by taking a break from the endless scrolling and comparing yourself to others, especially on image-based platforms. When you're constantly exposed to what others are doing, doubts about your own practice can creep in and freeze you in your tracks.

Maybe your witchcraft isn't as pretty or as organized as that of others. Maybe it isn't aligned with a specific popular aesthetic. So what? When you become obsessed with and involved in the doings of others, you forget who you are, what you are doing, and why you are here. It becomes a confusing distraction for your mind and drains your energy. Maybe you're the lucky one and these issues do not plague you. One thing is certain, however: Social media shapes our minds and our bodies for the worse. Take some time away to touch the soil. Sit under a tree. Connect with a friend. Read a book. Smell a rose. Plant some rosemary for remembrance and come into your practice. When you release superfluous distractions, a new light will shine on what really matters.

## When Opportunity Knocks, Open

Look for openings throughout your day and fill them with purpose. Notice where you find the opportunity to be in practice. Do you have an hour before you head to work? Maybe your evenings are free, but you regularly binge-watch a TV show. Maybe you're a little addicted to social media and spend inordinate hours scrolling. The point is, notice opportunities to reorient your priorities.

A simple way to reorient yourself is to write down your average day from waking to sleeping, including all that you do. Then take a good look at what is really necessary and what is unnecessary. Is there time in your day to make space for practice? Are you able to rearrange some things so you have an hour to sit and journal or pray? If your days are rushed and brimming with busyness, are you able to make time weekly? Even if it's just fifteen minutes for prayer, weave it in.

Use this as an opportunity to create space for your practice and to rework your schedule. If you don't have a schedule, take the time to create one. I understand that a "schedule" is something that many folks balk at. But I know that a schedule has saved my butt on more than one occasion. And creating a daily schedule can be a liberating practice. It helps you know what comes next and when to take a break. For me, creating a timeline of what to do with my day gives me structure that keeps me on task for things that are important to me and provides me with a sturdy foundation around which to orient my day. Your schedule needn't always be filled with "productive" activities. Schedule in a nap or rest. Leave time for reading, or for tending to your potted plants. This is your time; craft it as you wish.

## Learn to Recognize Ritual

Rituals are frequent acts that we take part in with regularity and consistency. It took me a while at the start of my practice to realize that I was already performing many small rituals throughout my day. Upon waking, I brewed a precious cup of coffee. Before retiring, I brewed a relaxing cup of herbal tea. I noticed that these were check-in points for me—times when I could reflect on myself and my life. Though seemingly mundane, they contained the elements of ritual and became magical for me. From there, I branched out and created a sequence of events that shifted my consciousness to take the next steps in my day.

Take a closer look at how you can create rituals throughout your day. You're probably already engaged in some! Do you make your bed or brew a cup of coffee or tea in the morning? Perhaps you brush your teeth every day or take an evening shower. These are daily rituals that you perform, often without even knowing it. Many of the magical moments you can access are right in front of you, and you can harness them to become more a part of your practice. All it takes is a little shift in perspective to make the mundane into magic.

For me, making tea or coffee first thing in the morning after making my bed signals that my morning practice of journaling, prayer, and spirit veneration has begun. The coffee or tea acts as an olfactory and sensory cue to enter my ritual space. In that space, I sit and journal, I ground and center, I pray and reflect. Notice the rituals you perform throughout your day and see where you can create space therein.

Journaling has become such a fruitful and important part of my witchcraft that I want to share more about it with you now, and encourage you to try the practice for yourself.

## A Magical Journal

Starting a magical journal in the space that you generate for your practice lets you focus on your calling and helps you figure out what is essential to your craft. Not only will this process be rewarding for you in the long run, it will also be immensely helpful for you and your process as you discover your path. A journal is a record that acts as proof of the efficacy of your magic. It validates your process and shows you where you are on your path.

When I first began journaling, I was nervous because I was intimidated by my shiny new notebook. I had no idea what I would write, so, with the first shaky stroke of my pen, I wrote down the date. Then I introduced myself: "Hello, I am Britton." I felt as if I were encountering a new person, and that perhaps that new person was me. But I was also recognizing that what I was going to write would become a physical artifact that would have the power to send ripples through the universe. It's true. When you write something down, especially your dreams and desires, they do gain more power to come true. With time and practice, my journal became a living spirit and a friend whom I encountered daily. Sometimes my entries were long; sometimes they were short. Often, I simply detailed the day's events or things I was thinking. Once I created the journaling habit, it stuck; on days when I did not write, I felt as if something were missing—like a visit from a good friend. Sometimes I let my journaling practice lapse, but I always come back to it, sometimes with an apology for being absent for so long.

Journaling has become, for me, a sacred ritual in which my ideas, thoughts, and encounters with spirit are recorded. I have even found that syncing my writing with the lunar cycles helps me record and remember. I have a ritual in which I write through the waxing, full, and waning moons. Then I review what I've written on the dark moon, starting a new cycle on the new moon. If you choose to do this, look for signs and patterns in your behaviors, thoughts, and dreams. It's in that reflection where I'm able to notice my own cyclical nature. Just like the moon, your writing may sometimes shine brightly; at other times, it may be so dim that it's barely perceptible. Developing your journaling habit may take time and patience, but I am certain it will be one of the most rewarding things you will ever do for yourself.

Journaling is simple. Just gather up a pen and a paper journal and write in your journal daily. You can find numerous beautiful "books of shadows" and "grimoires" out there in the witch world. But their sheer number can be overwhelming, leaving you with a sense of not knowing where to start. I recommend that you keep it simple. If you feel called to journal with paint or collage, or utilize other forms of artful recording, have at it. My point is that, once you create space for your practice, begin to journal in whatever way you wish.

The method presented in the practice below was developed by Julia Cameron in her book *The Artist's Way: A Spiritual Path to Higher Creativity*. She recommends writing three pages each day, in a stream of consciousness style. You can also use a set word count as a goal if you are working digitally. Julia stresses "no mental cigarette breaks!" Just let it all flow out. If you don't know what to write, simply write: "I don't know what to write." Something else will eventually bubble up to the surface. This type of writing can be a very revealing and rewarding process.

You don't have to follow this method, however. You can simply write a few pages however you wish. *Writing* is key here. Do not censor yourself. Keep pushing through any discomfort or nervousness, and you will find your flow. In the space you create for your practice, devote a half hour to an hour to journaling each morning, or whenever you wake up.

The following practice can help you warm up to journaling. The goal here is just to get you started so that you can discover your own magical efficacy and do some visioning for the future.

### Practice: Creating a Journal

If you're nervous about starting your journal, which I know many will be, begin with a simple introduction. Imagine you're sitting with a new friend and sharing stories, and simply answer the following questions:

- Who am I and where do I come from?

- What is my story and why am I here?

- What do I hope to achieve and experience in starting this new journey?

Imagine that you feel completely safe and comfortable in sharing your experiences and secrets with this new friend. Here's an example:

Hello, my name is Britton. I am thirty-six years old and originally from Georgia—I don't live there anymore. My father was in the military and that had me moving a lot as a child and teenager. Through my many journeys, I landed in the dusty high desert of eastern Oregon—the original lands of the Cayuse, Paiute, Umatilla, and Nez Perce people. I am surrounded by sagebrush and high mountains on all sides.

Check in with where you are *right now*. Don't look at what you lack; look at what you have and what you have generated for yourself. Ask yourself:

- Where have I made improvements in my life or made something I desired happen?

- Where have I overcome obstacles?

- Where have I empowered or transformed myself?

It may help to have a friend or someone who knows you well point out your own fabulous qualities and accomplishments. Friends and people we know and like often view us in beautiful ways that we never see ourselves. Your answers don't have to be elaborate; they can be as short or as long as you like. You may answer with something as simple as: "I learned how to cook myself a good meal." Or with a personal anecdote, like: "I can confidently wear bold red lipstick in public and I feel strong and sexy doing it."

Next, come into the present moment and pay attention to what surrounds you. Ask yourself:

- Where does the beauty in my path lie?

- What do I currently have to be grateful for?

- How have I helped to bring these things into my life?

- What can I do to manifest more beauty in my life and in the world around me?

And finally, explore how your practices as an earth witch can help you manifest more beauty and blessings on your own path and in the world at large. Ask yourself:

- What can I do in my practice to connect more regularly and more effectively with the spirits of the land and the natural world around me?

- What can I do in my practice to better understand what my plant and animal kin have to teach me?

- What can I do in my practice to reach out to my tree kin and hear the messages they offer me?

- What can I do to incorporate these messages into my path and my practice?

- How can I use this knowledge in ways that will benefit and protect the earth and the environment and all it contains?

The answers to these questions can bring about huge shifts in perspective and provide you with proof of your own magical efficacy.

Chapter 3

# Genius Loci

*A witch sees through things and around things. A witch sees
farther than most, a witch sees things from the other side. A
witch knows where she is, who she is and when she is.*
—Terry Pratchett

*Genius loci* is a term meaning "the prevailing character or atmosphere of a place," but it also refers to the
presiding god or spirit of a place. In classical Roman
religion, the genius loci were the protective spirits who
presided over places of power or where unique energy
resided. The Romans built shrines to honor them,
and we can still find some of these in our landscape
today—fountains where we toss coins, statues whose
patina has been worn to a bright sheen by those seeking blessings, groves of old trees, crossroads, and other
places of power.

Witches, above all, can recognize our inherent
connection to the land and its spirits. We are born

from this earth and supported by it. It is what grounds our practice. It is the place from which we may pivot. It is crucial to understand this because, as you begin exploring your spirit body and opening yourself up to spirit contact in the chapters to come, you will need to find a place to become rooted. That place will be the very ground upon which you stand—literally and metaphorically. It will be the environment with which you interact and the land by which you are informed. This rootedness will bring your awareness to the greater web of life around you and the unique ecology in which you participate.

The classic archetype of a witch is a person who lives just on the borders of civilization—someone both reviled and revered. Witches inhabit that strange and liminal space between what is wild and what is tame. There, they observe. In classical folk tales, witches are usually elderly, strange, or queer individuals who live in huts at the border of a town or village. They have knowledge of plants and animals, of the comings and goings of spirits, and of that which desires to remain hidden. They're also the ones who *know.* They are rooted in and connected to the web of life around them.

This archetype can still apply, however, even if you live smack-dab in the middle of a city. All space and land are sacred; there is no hierarchy of value here.

Land that has been tended with care and land that has been despoiled by extracting its resources are both sacred. If the land around you is in tatters and has been exploited to the extent that it is blasted and razed, don't judge it. Rather ask how you can help it. If you're standing in an old-growth forest, surely this is a special place. Ask how you can help protect it. How can you be of service?

The validity or value of witchcraft is not predicated on where witches live. It's their connection to that place that counts. Your connection to your surroundings is a part of your own *knowing* and your process of increasing your awareness and understanding. This is where the value lies—in your connection to your environment. Even if that connection feels uncomfortable or aloof to you—or sometimes even a little scary—it is still worth exploring. Having knowledge of your surroundings and still being willing to explore and understand them *is* the value.

It is crucial to your understanding that your actions be informed by the spaces you inhabit. I invite you to contemplate the following questions deeply:

- What do these spaces need and what is their resonance?

- What do I need and what is my resonance?

+ How do these two move through each other?
How does one inform and affect the other?

When I first came into my practice, I was not living in some ideal environment that offered me room to roam the countryside in search of places of power and uniqueness. I lived in a city, albeit a green and tree-laden city, and I feared that I would somehow be divorced from the magic of the earth.

As I began to awaken to my surroundings, I found myself reaching far and wide for connection to the land. During this time, I was without a car and often went to work or the grocery store on foot. I really didn't have a way to go outside the city limits into the forests to commune with nature, so I worked with what I had—the lichens and mosses growing in profusion along rock walls, the wild fruit trees that grew in alleyways, the weeds pushing up through cracks in the concrete.

If you look closely, you can find all that you need right in front of you. Spirit's presence can be experienced everywhere—even in sewers and powerlines, in busy city centers and back alleys, in dilapidated buildings and vacant lots. And your environment and what grows within it is often exactly the medicine you need in that moment.

## Animism

Animism (from the Latin word *anima*) means "breath," "spirit," or "life." Animism is the belief that *all* things contain a spirit or some form of animating life force, even seemingly inanimate objects like rocks, broken branches, old T-shirts, or pencils. For earth witches, it is the genius loci—the spirits of place—who animate the earth, giving the land and all it contains life and meaning and power. For them, rocks, plants, trees, insects, animals, seemingly inanimate objects, even the soil itself all hold resonances of place, origin, feeling, and spirit. This animistic worldview is crucial to our work as earth witches, because, in that work, we come into a relationship with all things—all living things and all things seemingly non-living.

Consider an object that you may take totally for granted, like an old wooden table. That table was hewn from a living tree that once stood in a forest. Imagine the experiences collected by this table in the places it may have inhabited and how it may be imbued with the qualities of those environments. Imagine seeing this table in all its unique character—the grain of its wood, the stains and scratches on its surface, its patina, and the feeling it impresses upon you. The table has a life. You may be able to gather a sense about where the wood has been and what it has seen. Perhaps you are repulsed by or deeply attracted to the table. You stand in relationship with it, whether you realize it or not. And with all that came before.

This table, like us in many ways, reflects its surroundings. It changes and influences us, and, in turn, also changes and influences our environment. Why would we limit this just to the human experience? Animism allows for personhood in the natural world, a world that our capitalist culture sees merely as something to exploit, to objectify, and to denude.

But witches shift this focus, and that shift is reflected in their language. When speaking of plant allies, for example, we change "*what* is that plant?" to "*who* is that plant?" By doing this, we open ourselves and others around us to a shift in perspective. For witches, all things are animate living beings that carry a spiritual pulse with which we may intertwine and interact. When we see a plant or flower that we are curious about, we open ourselves up to a much more living, embodied, and sensitive experience. We ask: "Who are you, and what is your power?" This question helps us cultivate a relationship based on curiosity and reciprocity. It becomes an invitation to connection, rather than a demand for a productive purpose.

If this is not already a part of your language, I invite you to try it. View the environment within which you live—a city, an urban landscape, a yurt in the woods, a mobile home, or an apartment in a small town—as inhabited by living, breathing beings with whom you can interact in subtle and not-so-subtle ways.

If this is a struggle for you, take a second look at the things around you right now in this moment. What memories are attached to them? Where did they come from? Can you trace their origin or maybe their story? Hold a few of these items if you can and experience them. What do you sense with your emotions? What do you feel in your body? Take note of these feelings. See if you notice anything about their spirit and what they want to share with you. What do they do? What is their function? How can you learn from them?

When you go outside, realize that your body and its magnetic field (essentially your heart's magnetic field) is encountering other beings who also radiate energy. It is in this special moment that you receive wisdom and guidance from them. It is then that you can respectfully and reverently interact with them. From there, you can really begin to cultivate your relationship to the land and the genius loci themselves.

## Deep Listening

Deep listening is a practice by which you can know and connect to both the land and the spirits you find there. Listening deeply requires generating stillness within and being in deep recognition of your surroundings. Meditation, grounding, centering, meditative walking, and deep observation of a particular place let you listen deeply and become more attuned to the messages the land or the objects you find there offer. They do not speak to you in your common language, but in the whispers of the wind, in the travel patterns of bees, in families of trees, in the texture of the dirt, and in the old structures that progress wants to knock down, perpetuating the myth that new is always better.

Deep listening is the language of naturalists—those who pay attention to the signs of nature. But earth witches take this listening a step further and interweave themselves with it all. They know we are not separate from nature or our surroundings, but an integral part of them.

Many years ago, in a late and dry summer, I took a trip to visit a coastal meadow that I loved dearly. It had been some time since I had been there. As I got out of my car, I could smell faint whiffs of wildfire smoke in the air, mingling with the salty air rolling in off the ocean. It was a strange contrast for a place known to be quite wet. I picked my way down a favorite trail to spend time with some plants whom I'd befriended on previous visits. The sky was a deep shade of blue, and the wind was ripping down the beach. A beautiful lighthouse stood at the tip of the cape, placed there to protect and guide ships. I wondered whether this would have been a place of power if civilization hadn't reached these shores. A place that *is* sacred—lighthouse or not.

I turned my gaze from the behemoth lantern toward the plants growing on all sides of the trail. Native salal berries mingled with grasses and wildflowers, some perhaps considered invasive, but persisting in the harsh environment. I noticed cut flower heads of yarrow. The farther I walked, the more evidence I saw that someone had come and snipped off every head without a care about the future generations of flowers, or the pollinators who needed them, or other folks who might also have wanted this medicine. An unease set in within me.

Crestfallen and disappointed, I decided to head to the windy beach. The wind ripped so ferociously that it tore off my ratty sweat-stained hat and it flew into a gulch. I gingerly found my way in and back out again, hat firmly in hand. I felt in my body that I needed to sit and to do some deep listening to hear what the place had to say, if anything.

I found a grassy outcropping right near a cliff on the edge of the ocean where the waves heaved and slapped the rocks. The beach there was desolate, with the bones of our earth and the bones of trees and of our civilization scattered all over it. Still alive yet quieter now, these natural artifacts had stories to tell—and I wanted to hear them. I settled near a large angelica plant—one known to protect and heal. This plant's large umbels reached up for the sky, and small pollinating bees rested in the flowers as the winds calmed and a soft breeze began to blow.

I reached down into the soil energetically. Dry grasses rattled around me, and the ground still held heat from the day's sun. It radiated up and warmed me. I cleared my mind as best I could, but all I could feel was stress. Tears began to flow as I let the sensations course through my body. The grasses, the hillsides, and other plants conveyed to me their own tension from a long bout of dryness, and I wondered how much of their stress I held in my own body and how much of mine they were holding. The sensations were mutual. The land was stressed and, in turn, so was I. I knew then how to be within the land, and I knew that what these plants needed was a gentle hand and gentle treading—to give and support, and not take.

Whoever had harvested that yarrow may have done so with good intentions, but now I understood that act wasn't necessarily welcomed by the land. If you have a friend who is stressed, wouldn't you want to ask how you could be of service? The land is not just a friend, but a lover—one we can look to with compassion and care. One with needs that we can listen to deeply. When we listen deeply and make that connection, we achieve a certain knowing that others do not have. We learn how to orient ourselves.

Before I left the beach, I made an offering of my hair for the land to remember me by and poured the remaining water from my canteen onto the ground. We must always notice and listen to the land that we inhabit and recognize our place within its ecology. We must always ask how we can be of service and do right by the spirits of the land with whom we're interacting. From there we can *know*, and the witch is one who knows.

Deep listening is not complicated, but it takes time and practice. Start by sitting or walking quietly in a space that calls to you. At first, your mental noise may be distracting. It often takes time to adjust from one space to another. Sometimes when I am rambling along my favorite trail, it takes a few miles of walking before I can tune in. All the natural world around me seems blurry and confusing for a moment, until I adjust from my previous civilized surroundings. Transitioning from our fast lives of cars and technology to something slower takes a moment. Allow it to happen. Take the space you need to tune in, and do not rush the process. You will arrive when you are meant to arrive.

Find a favorite spot and walk or sit with the land for a spell. Notice what you perceive, what comes up within you, and what you observe about the space you're occupying. Digest those sensations and let them rest deep within you as you take in the needs of your environment.

## Discovering Places of Power

Once upon a time, our ancestors venerated places of power, and some still do to this day. Nowadays, however, we often need to look with new eyes to discover the power that resides in the spaces around us. We must look where others might not, taking in small details as we learn the art of interpretation, and trusting our intuition as we gather more information.

Once when I was on a long, rambling hike along the Oregon coast, I stumbled upon a shrine to an indigenous woman. It was in a small clearing at the base of a long, narrow draw leading high up into the mountains of the coastal range. Around the shrine, I noted signs warning about trespassing and vandalism. Incredibly, some people were actually misguided enough to vandalize this sacred spot. As I approached the space, I noticed an intricate wooden statue of the woman, under which were many offerings. This was not only a place of power, but also one in which the story of an individual and her people was being honored.

In my pack, I had many beautiful stones that I'd gathered while walking along the beach. One, in particular, was very special to me—jasper and agate interwoven in the shape of an egg. I knew an offering had to be made, however, so I chose to offer this precious stone to her and to this sacred space. As I continued my walk, the space and shrine lingered with me for some time. Then it occurred to me, in the form of a deep sense of knowing at the center of my being, that she was the land's guardian spirit, and through grace and luck I had encountered this place of power.

Sometimes we stumble upon places of power in our wanderings, and sometimes we find them right under our noses. How do you find them? By wandering your landscape and locality and practicing deep listening. Go for a walk, shift your perspective, approach your environment with curiosity, and see what you can discover. Your eyes will tune into something different— something that most are not able or willing to see or that they take for granted. Maybe you already know a place of power that has been with you for some time.

Do you have a favorite hike? Maybe it is your favorite for a reason. Do you prefer one particular route in the city where you live for its beauty? There's probably something there worth exploring. Is there a particular patch of plants that you like to visit regularly? Check in with these spots, revisit them, and see what you perceive. Often, it is our bodies that tell us we've encountered a place of power. Sometimes, we just know and are in recognition of the sacred. A waterfall, a grove of trees, a river bend, a high desert peak, a stone outcropping—these powerful and sacred locations can be anything and everywhere.

Let your body be your point of contact—notice how you feel within. Move your consciousness to your heart space and be open to what surrounds you. Sometimes you may be overrun with chills or a warming sensation; sometimes the hair on the back of your neck may rise. Sometimes you may just be drawn to a particular space. Today's society encourages us to ignore these cues, or to think that they are foolish. And indeed, these cues have been and are actively being snuffed out. It is your ancestral right, however, to participate in this connection of feeling.

Recognizing places of power can clarify not just the landscape around you, but the powerful points and landmarks within that space. Take a field trip and see what you can find! All you need to do is step out your front door and go on an adventure to notice the power of the spaces around you. This not only deepens your knowledge of your environment; it also brings you into a deeper connection to it.

## Meeting Plant and Animal Kin

Growing up as a child in a military family, I moved around often and had to acquaint myself with new surroundings every few years. Little did I know then that I was building my own witch's toolkit within myself. Whether you've lived in single place all your life or have just recently moved, it's a valuable practice to reach out to the spirits who inhabit your surroundings.

Maps are a great tool to have as you start. Obtain a topographical map so that you can see the contours of your landscape. This can help you identify any peaks, draws, ravines, and bodies of water. Reviewing these maps can be a fun way to explore your area without even leaving your home. You can get great maps through your local state parks or forest service. You can even find them on the Internet. Maps can give you a bigger picture of the environment in which you live, and you can begin to orient yourself using the four cardinal directions: north, south, east, and west. Maps are a delightful way to take a mental adventure through your landscape.

Next, do a little research to find naturalist or plant guidebooks for your area. You can locate these at local bookstores, in your local library, or at local visitor centers. They often stock informational books on your area. Take your time to find books that are a good fit for you. While some may consider it cheating, you can also find plant-identification apps for your smartphone. Plant identification will be key to your work, as plants grow everywhere, and you'll want to get to know your fellow residents, as they play a very important role in your local ecology and in your journey. I recommend Thomas Elpel's book, *Botany in a Day: The Patterns Method of Plant Identification*.

As you explore, you'll quickly learn which plants are predominant in your area—the species that are most prolific there. If you live in a deciduous forest where many species abound, make note of the trees or shrubs that stand out the most to you. For example, I live in the high desert of eastern Oregon. Our most common tree species are conifers—pines, spruces, and firs. More specifically, Ponderosa pine, Douglas fir, and Engelmann spruce.

In your wanderings, you may also encounter what are known as "invasive" species, or plants like ornamentals that are not considered to be native to a particular region. Many look down on invasive species. But the truth is that they often work in mysterious ways that we do not yet understand. Some species help regenerate the soil and pave the way for new growth to occur. Others, like the invasive Himalayan blackberry of my region, provide food and shelter to birds, mammals, reptiles, and even humans. They often create massive barriers for land that needs to heal, or hold boundaries for land that may be vulnerable. This is a controversial view on invasives, but it's something worth looking at with different eyes.

While plants are often seen as stationary beings, because of rapid climate change, plants are on the move. Where certain plants may have thrived in a certain spot 100 years ago, they may not be able to thrive anymore, but may have become more suited to a different place. Nature, plants, and land are not fixed and static objects. They move, transform, and shift. These beings operate on a timescale to which we're not accustomed or that we don't even really completely understand. Often, restoration and conservation work seeks to return environments to the way they were *before* the climate began to change so rapidly, not to how they are in the present moment or will be in a shifting future. If you encounter these plant kin, be curious about them and what their role is in the environment's ecology. Their only crime is that they're thriving in a location where the powers that be have deemed them a threat to economic prosperity and expansion.

Once, I was obsessed with the herb Solomon's seal, which is used in folk magic to encourage wisdom and understanding. It was not native to the place where I lived at the time. I was frustrated, as I wanted to encounter this plant while it was thriving in the soil. One day during one of my long walks through the city, I found a massive patch of escaped Solomon's seal growing in a lush spot near a pedestrian overpass—they were everywhere! I was delighted to find these wild-growing magical roots. After spending some time with them, I harvested two roots and used them in my practice. The moral of the story? Don't overlook ornamental species or see them as invalid as you research your spirits of place.

Understanding who the animal inhabitants are in your location is also a great way to build your knowledge of the area's spirits. Connecting with our animal kin links us closer to the land and its cycles. What we learn from observing their behaviors and habits can inform how we, in turn, interact with the land, which is critical to an earth witch's practice. Wolves were one such creature with whom I was able to draw an observable connection. While living in my high-desert home, I'd heard rumors of wolves living there, and I confirmed those rumors through frequent sightings and, sadly, evidence of human predation. Anti-wolf sentiment runs high among ranchers whose lives depend on their herds. I discovered the importance of educational programs designed to teach the ranching community about the important role of the wolf in our local ecology. As earth witches, we can act in support of apex predators who need protection. We can vote to protect these beautiful beings and participate in programs to further our understanding of them.

## Stolen Land

We all live on stolen land in the United States. I come from an ancestry of colonial settlers, so it is important to me that I acknowledge that I live on land stolen from several different tribes. In your own exploration of connection to the land you live on, you *must* remember, understand, and support those who were there before you. Research tribes that live (or lived) in your area. Read their history from their perspective. As you read the history of these tribes, do so with a very critical eye. Much of it was written from the perspective of encroaching settlers. If ethnobotany—the study of the use of plants in folklore, medicine, magic, and religion—interests you, know that much of that knowledge was co-opted from oppressed people whom our government tried to eradicate.

Be sure to inform yourself about those who originally inhabited (and perhaps still inhabit) the land where you reside. Check out your local library or search the Internet for local tribal information. Knowing who the original stewards of the land are is critical, as you can look to them to lead the way in land restoration efforts. If possible, volunteer your time at a local community clean-up. Be of service to your environment. Being a witch means understanding who the original caretakers of the land are and supporting their efforts, even in seemingly "mundane" ways. Be sure to make this a part of your practice.

Many tribes have websites where you can obtain a list of native-owned businesses to support. Give your spare dollars to indigenous artists, activists, and communities. This is an important way in which you can connect with and honor the spirits of the land. We are all children of this earth, and it is our sovereign human right and obligation to interact with the land in respectful and reverent ways. Understanding the original stewards of the land can only serve to deepen your understanding of the landscape itself. Learn about and respect the culture and sacred sites of those who came before you. If you're going to interact with the landscape, you must know your own place in it.

## Connecting with Spirit

Being familiar with the spirits of the land you inhabit is a perfect way to begin connecting with and understanding the landscape around you. Then you can further your connection to the land through offerings, divinations, and other practices. There are many ways to do this, and we'll look at some of them in the coming chapters.

For now, I encourage you to develop and listen to your intuition as you practice. When sitting with or visiting a piece of land with whose spirits you feel a connection, simply ask if they have a message for you, or what they might like as an offering. Often, this intuition arrives as a message that feels as if it comes from outside you. I have heard it described by many as something just dropping in—like a droplet of water that creates ripples in the pool of your mind and heart. This knowing comes from both within and without. It merges with you as you merge with the land and with spirit.

Of course, intuition is by definition deeply personal, so I cannot tell you how these messages will look for you on your journey. My best advice is to listen deeply to your innermost thoughts. A meditation practice (see page 66) or a grounding and centering practice (see chapter 4) can help you get in touch with your intuition. Learning to differentiate between your thinking mind's voice and the voice of that which surrounds you takes time, patience, and practice. Don't worry, it will come to you naturally over time.

If you feel unsure about the messages you receive, you can perform an experiment. Say you feel as if a tree is asking for an offering from you, but you're unsure if it's your mind speaking or the tree. Follow through on the offering and see what comes of it. Much of a witch's practice is based on doing. Without action, magic is not worked. Better to do the magic than not. It is how you gain experience—by doing. Learning how to differentiate between the voice of your mind and the voice of the land is another aspect of the deep listening I spoke of. Stick with it and soon it will become natural to you.

## Offerings

And finally, when it comes to making offerings to the land, I would be remiss if I didn't remind you to be sure that your offerings do not cause harm to the environment. Too often, I have found the remains of offerings that do not break down or cannot be consumed by the earth—like plastics and glitter. Use sound judgment in whatever you choose to leave as an offering.

When I was getting to know elder trees near my home, it took me a while to court them—just as you would do if you were sweet on someone. A full year passed before I ever harvested any of their medicine. I left cream, honey, and strands of my hair as offerings. I harvested only after I felt I had established a mutual connection of reciprocity and received the message: "You may gather from me." Now, I always make offerings whenever I harvest, often leaving them at the largest tree in the area. Some spirits command a lot of coaxing and tending, and this is the case with elder trees. However, some plants, like dandelions, are quite giving. It all depends on the individual nature and personality of the spirit.

Good basic offerings to start with are hair, honey, milk, and cream, as they are sweet and gentle. Use caution around what are called "hot" offerings like alcohol, caffeine, or blood. Be sure that you know what the spirit wants. Hot offerings can really activate spirits and "rile them up," so to speak. Stick with gentle or "cool" offerings when you're first starting out—items like gentle incenses and sweet and basic foods with a minimum of hot spices. One of the best ways to charm spirits is with sweets. This is a gentle and friendly way to get to know them. Tobacco can be helpful as well, as it helps establish an atmosphere of communication and connection. I often use it as an offering with trees, along with honey. Think about the kinds of gifts we give to our human loved ones. We give cookies and bake cakes; we offer favorite foods; and sometimes we share tobacco as a bonding experience. These are the types of cool offerings that the spirits love.

How do you make an offering? Just hand it over. For plants and trees, simply place the offering near their base. For animals, simply place the offering where you know they feed. For ancestors, you can locate your offerings on a dedicated altar or shelf in a sacred part of your home. Offer your gifts to them in the same way that you would offer them to a friend or loved one. Perhaps take a moment to listen after making the offering to see if anything is communicated to you through your intuition, your mind's eye, or other pathways.

### Practice: Nature Inventory

This practice will help you get to know the plant and animal kin that inhabit the landscape in which you live, as well as the major features of that landscape and its original stewards. This is something everyone can do, whether you live in the city or in the country. And your first step is right outside your front door, however that looks for you.

So let's gear up and go! Grab your favorite comfortable walking shoes, a pen and notebook (or your witch's journal), and maybe a little pack with some snacks. And don't forget your water! You're going on an adventure. Here's an outline you can use as a guide.

Write down each of these as you encounter them on your walk, or as you discover them through books and learning about your area:

Predominant tree species: _____

_____

Predominant shrub species: _____

_____

Predominant herbaceous plant species ("weeds"): _____

_____

_____

Apex predators: _____

_____

Large mammals: _____

_____

Small mammals: _____

_____

Reptiles: _____

_____

Insects: _____

_____

Major landmarks (rivers, rock formations, mountains, hills, etc.): _____

_____

Indigenous peoples and tribes of your area: _____

_____

_____

As you become more familiar with the non-human kin who populate the land around you, reach out to their spirits and begin to connect more intimately with them. As you begin to receive messages from them, work to integrate them into your practice in ways that benefit the earth.

### Practice: Walking Meditation

Meditation, the act of quiet contemplation, can be a powerful tool for calming the noise of life so you can listen deeply to the earth. A walking meditation can turn an ordinary stroll into a direct experience and appreciation of the land and the life that abounds there. By simply focusing your attention on your surroundings and opening yourself to what you observe, you invite the life force of the earth to flow around and within you.

Walking meditations can be particularly useful to you as an earth witch, because they engage you directly with the environment. With your eyes wide open and moving at a pace that suits you, you can connect to all that surrounds you through your physical body and your senses, and immerse yourself in the present moment.

All you need to perform a walking meditation is a place in nature where you feel safe and can wander undisturbed. This can be a park near your home, a favorite stretch of beach, a nature preserve, a mountain trail, or a forest. It can even be your own backyard. Anywhere where you can connect directly to your surroundings and commune with the spirits of place. The unique benefit of a walking meditation, compared to a seated meditation, is that, rather than focusing on just your breath, it engages your entire body in physical activity and draws on all your senses.

You can even perform a walking meditation in the hustle and bustle of a city. An urban environment may have more distractions, true, but that doesn't mean that you can't be mindful of the world around you. In fact, if you are a city-dwelling witch, your mind is likely to be more stimulated than it would be in the stillness of a natural landscape, so there's even more reason for you to ground yourself in the earth and reach out to your spirits of place.

Before you begin, consider ways that you can heighten your experience. Are there certain trees or plants or animals whom speak to you regularly? If so, bring small offerings to give them in return for their care. Is there specific guidance you seek for your life right now? Are there questions you want answered or specific messages you want to receive? If so, let these guide you.

As you enter the space in which you have chosen to wander, immerse yourself fully in it. Let it interact with your body. Let it penetrate your senses. As you walk, notice how your body feels. Does it feel heavy or light? Stiff or relaxed? Take note of your posture and your gait. Don't try to change them, just observe them. Let the rhythm of your movement become a gentle point of focus.

Now tune in to what's going on around you. Is the sun low on the horizon? High in the sky? Do you see animal kin scurrying about or insects swirling through the air? Are there rocks, or trees, or plants inhabiting this space? What smells are you breathing in? Are they pleasant? Unpleasant? Do they call up memories or associations in your mind? Is it windy? Breezy? Calm? Is the air soft and warm? Damp and misty? Cool and crisp? How does it feel on your face?

As you walk, let the rhythm of your own movement bring you into an awareness of the rhythms of the environment around you. Feel yourself become grounded in the soil beneath your feet. Take note of its texture. Is it damp? Dry? Wet? If the ground is strewn with rocks or pebbles, can you feel their resonances? Do they have any messages for you? Notice what you are feeling, but don't judge any feelings that arise. Just let your body interact with your surroundings. If you feel your mind becoming distracted, gently bring your attention back to the sensation of the earth beneath the soles of your feet.

Now take note of the plant kin you see as you walk. Are there trees around you? If so, are they mature trees? Seedlings? Are they in bud? In full leaf? Are their branches bare? What species are they and what significance does this have for you in your practice? Are they tall, stately pines, or soft yellow-green birches? Reach out to them and ask if you can harvest a twig, a leaf, or a bit of bark to carry with you or place under your pillow as a reminder of their strength. If they agree, leave offerings at their roots or in a convenient hole or notch. Are there mosses or lichen growing on their trunks? If so, think about this symbiotic relationship and what it means for the health of the land as a whole.

Are there flowers in bloom—daffodils or daisies or lavender? Is the air heavily scented with their blossoms? Are there herbs that are ready to be harvested—skullcap or mugwort or peppermint? If so, consider how you can use their medicine in your practice. Are there grasses moving gently in the breeze? If so, what are they whispering to you? Are there bees busily pollinating the plants you see? If so, what does this teach you about the life of the earth and your place in it?

If you are walking a favorite beach, are the waves rolling softly or breaking noisily on the shore? Is the tide rising or receding? Is the sand littered with shells or washed clean? Perhaps you see gulls riding the air currents high above the waves and hear their raucous calls. Consider what lessons you can learn from all these energies and how you can apply those lessons in aid of the earth.

If you are finding your way through a forest, does the light filter through the tree tops and throw dancing shadows at your feet? What sounds are drifting into your consciousness? Do you hear bird song? If so, consider what message it may be sending you and how you can share that message with others. If you can, sit on the ground and lean back against a tree, aligning your spine with its trunk. How does this affect your relationship with the tree?

As you immerse yourself fully in the richness of the land around you, see yourself as fully in your power as you practice your craft. Breathe in the presence of the spirits of the land and invite them into your life. Experience your own power as a part of the natural world.

When you are finished with your walk, send a pulse of thanks downward into the soil from your heart, through your spine, and finally through your feet. When you return home, be sure to capture your experience in your journal, recording all the thoughts, feelings, and emotions that came to you during your time of connection so you can return later to review them, especially when you feel you have strayed from your path.

Chapter 4

# Earth, Trees, and the Body

*Never permit a dichotomy to rule your life, a dichotomy
in which you hate what you do so you can have pleasure in
your spare time. Look for a situation in which your work
will give you as much happiness as your spare time.*
—Pablo Piccaso

We are of the earth, and the relationship we have with
our physical bodies provides a secure place from which
we can begin to explore the world of spirit. Our physical bodies are our homes. They are the means by which
we are embodied on this earth. But they are also part
of our spiritual bodies and thus can provide us with
access to the spirits who inhabit both our world and
other worlds. As earth witches, this sacred access is
always available to us through our bodies.

It is important, therefore, that, as we listen to the
earth and the spirits we discover there, we listen as
well to our own bodies, as doing so can teach us many
things. Ultimately, it is through our bodies, through

our senses, that we experience this world and the unseen worlds around us. And by cultivating a relationship to our bodies, we open a portal to spirit.

Perhaps the most harmful idea society perpetuates about our bodies is also the most subtle. In our Western culture, both religion and philosophy tell us that there is a *division* between the material and the spiritual worlds, and consequently that our bodies, which are of the earth, are somehow *less than* and *not* spiritual. But I am here to tell you that there is no such hierarchy—that our bodies, which are of the earth, are also of the spirit. It's only our culture that makes the mistaken distinction.

To overcome this dualistic view of body and spirit, one of the big hurdles that many of us need to overcome is to love our bodies exactly as they are in this moment. Most of us are taught to do the opposite. We have a mental list of things we don't like about our bodies, that we wish we could change, or that we may even hate. Today, shame and thoughts that our bodies are unworthy are at epidemic levels.

That's not surprising when you consider that this kind of negative thinking has been impressed upon us by a toxic culture. Since birth, we've been taught not to trust and love our bodies. We have been conditioned to think that we need something outside of ourselves for our bodies to be whole and complete, and we are taught to seek things outside ourselves to mend the connection to our own bodies. This is an easy trap to fall into in a capitalist culture where we are taught to believe that the next thing we purchase will bring us happiness and cure our woes and ills.

In my own case, I spent many of my early years on my path feeling strangely guilty about desiring a deeper connection to myself, to my own intuition, and to my spirituality. It took some time to unravel this guilt and, to this day, I am still doing the work of unlearning and relearning. If this is something with which you struggle, you are not alone. But the very fact that you are reading this book shows that you are willing to undergo a process of transformation and to bridge the false gap between body and spirit that our culture has created.

In fact, it is only through our bodies and the senses available to us that we can experience the elements of our world viscerally. One of the gifts of witchcraft is that we come into a deeper sense of knowing through sight, through the vibration of sound and hearing, through mind-altering smell, and through the sensuousness of touch. Awakening or reawakening our awareness to these stimuli and the parts and aspects of ourselves that experience them aren't just mundane experiences. They remind us that we are animals, with instincts and intuitions to guide us that are informed through these sensations and their subtleties. If this isn't spiritual, I don't know what is.

Many of us who experience a strong call to find our spirituality may notice that the precursor or initiator of this experience is pain, trauma, radical transitions, and/or illness, and that these initiators show up in myriad ways. Indeed, these often are and can be a part of *feeling the call* to become a witch and awakening to witchcraft. And this call may not always be very pleasant. The wounds inflicted by society often inform the healing in the call to witchcraft, and this healing opens us up to the unique individual gifts we have as earth witches.

When we begin the process of coming into our bodies and stimulating greater awareness there, we open up to the possibility that the physical world is actually a world of spirit. When we weave this new awareness into the animism discussed in chapter 3, we really begin to dissolve the idea that the magical and the mundane are separate from each other. We begin to deconstruct the notion that we are somehow always in a state of separateness from the sacred. In fact, as witches, our inherent animism implies that we have a basic respect for and relationship to the things around us—including the land, trees, plants, rocks, and everything that surrounds us.

To understand this better, let's take a deeper look at trees, as they can also be potent allies in helping us access the body and its connection to the spirit world.

## The Importance of Trees

Trees may be the single most important species on our planet, as they provide over a quarter of the life-giving oxygen that all creatures, including humans, need to survive. They give shelter to animals and nourishment to insects. They regulate the fertility of the soil by maintaining proper levels of nutrients. They absorb greenhouse gasses and help to preserve groundwater resources. And they play an important role in regulating the temperature of the entire planet.

Moreover, recent research by University of British Columbia professor and ecologist Suzanne Simard has shown that trees are *social* creatures. They communicate with each other. Trees, she explains, are linked to neighboring trees by an underground network of colorful fungi that resembles the neural networks in the brain. Trees actually organize themselves into communities around what Simard calls "mother trees" that act as a nexus for the sharing of information and nutrients important to the health of the whole forest. And this networked communication holds important implications for us as earth witches.

My own first deep experience with a tree was with a red alder in my surbuban backyard. The tree was gnarled and old for a fast-growing alder. They don't tend to live very long as far as trees go, usually only about 100 years. I was very drawn to this swampy, water-loving tree. Many of its branches were dead and dripping red sap like blood. Its leaves were deeply veined and, as I studied the species, I found that their medicine works on our lymphatic system and the waters and fluids of the body. I also learned that they are a tree of the Otherworld.

In the early stages of my witchcraft, I'd learned that witches and shamans visited the Otherworld through portals like groves of trees, bramble thickets, tree roots, and other places of power. One night, I dreamed that I approached this red alder and found a hole just at its base that was intertwined with roots and leaves. I slipped into the hole and found myself in a tunnel. Then I walked out of the tunnel and through a bramble thicket that opened into a forest. This humble and common tree had taught me how to access the Otherworld.

And I did not need to go to this tree in its physical form to enter this other realm. The anatomy of the tree mimicked my own, and my spine, like the trunk of the tree, was indeed an access point within myself. My relationship to this tree taught me much, including how to travel within and outside of the body. This revelation reminded me of the belief in the World Tree, a common tradition in European and northern European shamanism that is also found across many, if not all, cultures in different guises.

The World Tree is the pole that runs from the lower worlds to the upper worlds. Also referred to as the World Pillar or *Axis Mundi*, it is the connection between heaven and earth, between earthly and celestial realms, between heaven and hell, between canopy and root. The World Tree helps give definition to both our spiritual selves and the parts of the Otherworld to which we may travel. It helps us ground and center ourselves, and connects us more deeply to both the earth and spirit. The roots of the tree represent the Lower World. The trunk and lower branches support the Middle World. And the top of the tree's canopy defines the Upper World.

In the context of the soul and consciousness, the Upper World relates to the heavens, the higher self, and the super-consciousness. The Middle World represents the earth, the waking self, and the waking consciousness. The Lower World comprises the lower self, and the unconscious or shadow. However, this analogy to aspects of the self and consciousness, while enlightening, is not absolute. For example, your lower self, your shadow, isn't the actual Lower World, nor does it even live there. The shadow self lives within you, and you have access to the Lower World through your body. The Lower World itself is an actual realm of spiritual and elemental forces. However, some likeness does exist between those things.

I understand this may seem a little abstract. Just think of it as a reflection of the famous axiom of Hermes Trismegistus, teacher of high magic and alchemy: "As above, so below; as within, so without; as the universe, so the soul." The three parts of the World Tree simply represent the three parts of our soul and consciousness, and they all reflect each other in an interesting and harmonious way. The important thing is to realize that the World Tree exists both inside of us, in our bodies, and outside of us.

As a cosmological view, the World Tree can provide us with a framework for doing deeply personal transformative work within ourselves, connecting us to both our bodies and the earth. It enables us to move through the Otherworld. This is also known as "walking the hedge," journeying, and spirit flight. With

time—with baby steps and practice—you will be able
to do these things.

## The Spirit Body

As I mentioned earlier in this chapter, our physical
bodies are both connected to and inform our spirit
bodies. I must warn you, however, that the anatomy of
the spirit body can be difficult to describe. My understanding of it was informed by the work of American witch and co-founder of the Feri tradition, Victor
Anderson, author of *Etheric Anatomy: The Three Selves
and Astral Travel*.

Feri is a tradition of North American witchcraft
that emphasizes awareness and sensual experience. In
my practice, this tradition has been immensely helpful in understanding how parts of my spirit interact
with the living world my body inhabits, and with the
Otherworld. If this doesn't align with your personal
understanding of your spirit body, however, I completely understand, as there are a multiplicity of views
on this subject. In my own case, the Feri tradition has
shown me how the different parts of our spirit body
work, and how we set these parts in motion. As we
go forward, I invite you to consider how this understanding might apply for you. For instance, if it feels
uncomfortable at first, that may be because parts of

your spirit body have been long neglected (usually the shadow or lower self).

The Feri tradition recognizes three essential parts of the spirit body—consciousness, or the waking self; the shadow, or the lower self; and super-consciousness, or the higher self. The conscious or the waking self is the part of you that is mentally processing the words you're reading right now. This is the part of you that makes your coffee, goes to work, engages in conversations, and thinks thoughts. The ego—the mediator between the person and reality—is part of your conscious self.

Your lower self, sometimes called the shadow self, is your unconscious, primal, and instinctive self. Your shadow self is part of your unconscious mind, which is comprised of impulses, repressed ideas, and embarrassing fears and tendencies. The beliefs that are buried there can cause you to react to certain situations instead of responding. "Why do I always do that?" is a refrain often heard from people who "self-sabotage." The answer to that question is often found in the beliefs of the shadow self. Carl Jung, famous 20th-century psychoanalyst, pointed out the importance of this part of the spirit body: "Until you make the unconscious conscious, it will direct your life and you will call it fate."

Some witchcraft traditions call this part of the spirit body the "fetch," which is a part of you, but is also its own self. The fetch is possibly related to your *daemon*, a personal spirit that comes to you at birth. You are most connected to your fetch when you are a child.

For witches, fetches take the shape of animals or creatures. They are our chief familiars. They go and "fetch" information for us. I personally believe that my fetch lives at my heart center, attached to me by an etheric cord—an emotional energy connection. I inhabit this part of myself when traversing the other worlds. My fetch comes to me in animal form, giving me information and showing up in my dreams. Some describe it as the etheric body—the part of us that engages in astral travel or out-of-body experiences.

Fetches are sometimes suppressed and shamed into hiding, so it may take years to connect with yours. Do not rush to get to know exactly how your own fetch takes shape. For now, imagine it as a white and light-blue ball of light until it reveals itself to you in time. Respect the time it takes for your fetch to reveal itself and relax into knowing that you're working to bridge the gap between you and this part of your spirit body.

The irony is that understanding your lower self also offers the fastest pathway to your higher self, as they communicate with each other quite easily. This communication is how you begin to integrate your shadow self. Your higher self resides in the space just above your head, connecting to the base of your neck. This is where spirit may enter you. Also known as the "godhead," this is your direct connection to however your "god" appears to you. The godhead is where you receive the divine essence and can connect to a higher consciousness. When you receive these "downloads" or intuitive messages, they arrive via your godhead. Connection or integration with your lower self—your shadow and your fetch—can help clarify these messages.

You aren't meant to master all of this overnight. Allow this information to sink in over time. Focus on your fetch, your lower self, and your shadow. Our shadows hold many dark desires, and the key is not to shame them, but to invite them in and give them deep approval. Hold them in the deepest of love—claws, fangs, and all.

## The Spine and the Spirit Body

Most of us know the physical importance of our spine. It carries information from the brain to all other parts of the body. But your spine is also the gateway to the Otherworld—it acts like the Axis Mundi, or the World Tree we spoke of in the previous section. It's the built-in system that connects you to spirit. Your spine is the trunk of your tree (body) and, from it, you can move your spirit and energy from top to bottom, and back up from the Lower to the Upper World.

Connecting your spine to the generally gentle and friendly ally spirit of a tree not only enables you to explore other realms, but also to sense and feel into spirits who interact with you. This connects you more deeply with your spirit body. Having a strong and active bodily connection lets you go deeper into this work with a sense of safety, especially if you're wandering around the Otherworld and want to know how to return to your body. This sense of safety can prove useful during deep dreamwork, where you may sometimes feel lost or trapped within your dreams.

This is another reason loving your body, exactly as it is, is so important to your practice. When you feel in touch with and in connection to your body, you can return to it with ease and security. That's why I stress a bodily acceptance and movement practice, as it can teach you how to be *in* the body and to love it. The grounding and centering practice below can help you make and maintain that connection. It teaches you how to connect with earthly and celestial realms. It helps you move into the earth, draw up energy, and ascend to the heavens, then bring down energy to create a circuit within your body. This helps you create a boundary that you can erect to carry with you through your day. While this ritual may seem long, it's actually quite a quick process once you get the hang of it.

### Practice: Grounding and Centering

Settle yourself quietly in a comfortable sitting position. If you can, sit directly on the ground and not in a chair. It's important here to keep your spine upright and erect, but do whatever is most comfortable for you and your body. You can lean against a wall for support and/or place a cushion or pillow under you if needed.

Begin by taking a few deep breaths. Feel into your body and bring your awareness to your spine. Visualize being able to move up and down it energetically. As you do so, move your energy into your pelvic bowl where your "root," your energetic connection, begins.

Send your roots down into the soil like a tree or a plant. You may need to pass through the wood of your floor and the concrete of a city full of steel beams and sewers. You can pause here in these places to feel what they're about if you like. Move farther downward until you hit the soil. Feel its texture. Is it cool and damp? Warm and dry? Are you crossing paths with a nearby tree, plant, man-made structure, or mycelial network? If so, appreciate them by giving them a nod.

Keep moving downward. You may begin to push through solid rock, a water table, or an aquifer. Keep moving down, down, and down.

Eventually, it will begin to grow hot and the earth may rumble. Keep moving until you reach an orange-red heat. Pass through it until you've found the white-hot core—the heartbeat of the earth that sustains all life on our planet. It is pulsing.

Give thanks for the earth's heartbeat and share any words you feel compelled to speak. From here, draw the earth's energy back up into your body. It is snake-like and red. Allow it to fill you completely, from your toes to the crown of your head. Sit here in appreciation for a moment if you like.

Now, begin moving energy upward. Eventually, move up through your roof or whatever is located above you. Move into the sky and the atmosphere. Is it raining? Are you passing through clouds? Is it morning or nighttime? In which direction is the sun? Where is the moon? Continue moving upward until the sky gives way from blue to black and is flecked with stars and planets. Reach out to your star kin or any heavenly body to which you feel called. Touch in with them and yourself here. Give thanks and share any words you feel compelled to speak.

Bring the celestial light of your star kin and the moon downward into the crown of your head. It is dovelike—the color a glimmering silvery white. Allow this glorious light to fill your whole body, mingling with the red serpentine energies you gathered from the earth.

Now, place your palm over your heart and your other hand on top of it. Gather these energies together at the center of your heart. Watch them form into a ball that encapsulates your heart, then have this ball of energy expand into an egg-like shape that surrounds your whole being. It may be light-golden in color or whatever color it manifests for you. Set this capsule with an intention to protect you, calling on any guardian spirits you wish to help as needed.

This capsule will serve as a protective energetic barrier with flexible boundaries. You do not want to create hard and brittle boundaries—they must flex with the environment you inhabit. Be thankful for this layer of protection and say a prayer of thanks to any guardian spirits involved and for the energy your environment has given you.

This practice will most likely not look the same for you as it does for me. Your own experiences will surface here, as you have your own inclinations and preferences. And that is how it should be.

*Practice: Accessing the World Tree*

To begin this practice, find a tree that you can connect with within a safe space—in your backyard, a local park, a nature preserve, any place that feels safe to you. You will know the tree when you find it, as this is where the deep listening comes in.

Next, do some research. Come to understand your tree's ecological role and growth patterns. Is it a native species? (This does not matter, but it's good to know.) Do some folkloric research on the species to understand how and why it is important in a folkloric sense. Is it protective? Does it have a reputation for being a tree that helps facilitate exploration to other realms? Does it have a medicinal quality?

Begin to forge a relationship to this tree by making frequent visits and leaving offerings. Sit with the tree. I find it helpful to place my back against the tree's trunk and align my spine with the spine of the tree. From there, you can perform a grounding exercise to meet with the tree's roots. Leave offerings at the roots or in a convenient hole or notch. Honey, hair, or bits of sweet foods are good offerings with which to start. Carry a leaf, a twig, or a bit of the tree's bark near your body or sleep with them under your pillow. Touch and speak to them. Ask what they want for future offerings. Invite the tree completely into your life.

When you have found your tree and have developed a relationship with it, try the grounding practice above while sitting at its base. This can bring you into further spiritual alignment with your tree.

*Practice: Know Your Body*

It is important to engage your body in ways that are safe and interesting to you. This can help you discover what gifts you hold within your body and where you struggle the most. Often, the struggle point can be a great place of exploration and can build character.

Engaging in a movement practice can begin to open you up to a greater connection to your body and the resonances it carries. Your movement should suit you as an individual. It should stimulate your body and move it out of a cerebral place and into your instinctual, felt self. Here are some options:

- Simple breathing exercises

- Yoga

- Self-pleasure (having orgasms)

- Powerlifting (my personal favorite)

- Walking

- Running

- Riding a bike

- Dancing

- Mobility exercises

- Gardening

- Playing and/or creating music (very much an embodied practice)

- Crafts involving the hands and body, like knitting, basket weaving, painting, or creating any art

Use this list as a starting point to find what works best for you and what resonates with your body and proclivities. Any movement of the body that works for you and feels sustainable can get you out of your head and into your body and deeper states of awareness.

If you're exploring a movement or embodiment practice that is new to you, it may take some time for muscle memory or a comfortable and relaxed state to develop so that you can make the shift from a cerebral state into a state of body awareness. This may be a little difficult at first. Don't give up immediately. Give yourself the time and space needed for the practice to take shape.

Be gentle on yourself and challenge yourself where you feel called to do so. Witchcraft will move you into many uncomfortable moments and facing your physical discomforts (within reason) can become a valuable experience that informs your practice.

# Chapter 5

# The Cycles of the Earth

*If I believe in anything, it would be nature—trees,*
*clouds, rain—the life cycles that begin and end, season*
*after season. That makes sense to me—nature as God.*
—Ellen Wittlinger

In our society today, "progress" is seen as linear. We are constantly encouraged to get better, to do more, to make more, to have more, to be more, as if we are eventually going to reach some imaginary Utopia where everything is perfect.

This linear concept of progress is a fantasy of the human ego, as nothing in nature works in this fashion. Instead, nature shows us the power of cycles. There is no linear progress in nature, but rather a continuous process of birth, death, and rebirth, in a beautiful rhythm that invites us to just be and experience the grandeur of it all.

Because witchcraft teaches us that we are, after all, of the earth, it also invites us to reflect and embrace these rhythms. As we move through the days, weeks, and seasons, each carries its own peculiar quality. As we move through the moon's many phases, they reflect our own phases. And seasonal cycles invite us to live more deeply connected to the earth, the moon, and the stars. By living with more awareness of these cycles, we can see how they guide and shape our lives.

The seasons of the year can act as cues for us. In summer, we gather experiences and growth. We bloom into the fullness of our expression. In winter, we slow down and hibernate in warmth and tend the seeds that we carry from the fall. In spring, the sap moves, and we stir from winter hibernation into new and exciting activities, and those seeds we nurtured begin to grow.

Living in rhythm with the seasons is a lot easier than some may think. All you have to do is simply go outside and pay attention. In this chapter, I'll show you ways to explore these cycles and how to connect to them. My approach may seem a little unconventional, however. I want you to connect to the seasons *in the location in which you live*. Because of this, we will not be working with the traditional Wheel of the Year.

The traditional Wheel of the Year comprises an annual cycle of seasonal festivals that are based on European pagan and folk practices that mark and celebrate the turning of each season. Many of the "witches' holi-days"—like Beltane, Lammas, Imbolc, and Samhain—are based in these traditions. But, while beautiful and inspiring, these festivals don't always line up with our own spirits of place. In some ways, I feel we do the land and the locations we inhabit a disservice by applying a ritual framework that is foreign to them and therefore rather incomprehensible to the spirits of place themselves. These festivals may apply if you live in the British Isles or in parts of Western Europe where much of the traditional Wheel of the Year is grounded. But they don't necessarily connect us to the reality of our own experience of the unique and varied places in which we live. If you live in Western Europe, the Wheel of the Year may very well work for you. But we need to discover our own ebbs and flows and how they're connected to the cycles of the land we inhabit.

In witchcraft, there are various ways to celebrate, honor, and pay heed to seasonal shifts, and they don't all necessarily align with the older traditions. The seasons and patterns of Ayrshire, Scotland, may not look like the seasonal patterns of say, Tucson, Arizona. I invite you to take a bioregional and animistic view of how you notice seasonal shifts and patterns, rather than concen-trating on the framework and traditions of a location to which you may not have a direct connection.

In my early days of witchcraft, I was very eager to follow the Neopagan Wheel of the Year by rote. And that worked for me for a time. While I was living in the lush rain forests of western Oregon, where the climate is quite similar to that of the British Isles and parts of Western Europe, winter still held a lot of green life, as lichens, mosses, and ferns still thrived and even brightened in the depths of winter. Spring usually arrived on time and was fully alive in April. In July and August, the environment began to dry out and fruits ripened, and the harvest season lined right up with Lammas, the first day in August. It was a beautiful and solidifying experience to follow these seasonal shifts, and I loved honoring them.

However, when I reflected on my childhood in southern Florida, it made me wonder: How would this work *there*? Winter in Florida is almost imperceptible. The climate there seems to be a constant state of spring- and summer-like conditions. I wondered how I would apply the Neopagan Wheel of the Year in a place where it wasn't really relevant.

When I relocated to the high desert, I knew that following these traditional cycles was not going to work, so I paid attention to the environment around me. Spring doesn't fully activate here until late May, and fall arrives a bit earlier. The summers are dry and hot, and even mimic a sort of inverse winter, as plants die back and go dormant. Winter is long in the high valley where I live, and even longer when you climb high up into the mountains. Sometimes snow falls well into July. In spring, I religiously take long walks in the sagebrush to look for one flower, the sagebrush buttercup—my harbinger of spring. When I see them blooming, I know for sure that we are likely to have one or two more light snows, followed by a warming cycle that then initiates the growth of all the wildflowers on the sagebrush steppe. That is my celebration, my spring rite—the blooming of a single flower species.

When you look and pay attention, you can find the signs and signals of seasonal change all around you. You don't need preordained structures. What flower blooms first in the spring where you live? Which flowers bloom as summer ends and fall begins? Which plants leaf out first in the spring? When does the snow start to melt? When do you notice certain bird songs that come and then disappear seasonally? All these things will be totally unique to your area, and that is beautiful and magnificent. This defines your wheel of the year.

Another aspect of this equation is climate change. As I write this book, the northwestern United States has experienced the hottest summer on record.

Temperatures of 117° in parts of the Pacific Northwest were previously unheard of. Change is happening—and it is rapidly affecting our plant kin and their ability to thrive. In my region, spring, while not early, has become very short. Most plants have become stunted or very limited, because they are reserving their energy and protecting themselves. We've barely had any rain of which to speak. Fruits came a whole month early, as did huckleberries, one of my favorite foods.

What does this mean for an earth witch's practice? It's hard to tell, as these changes are happening so quickly. But as witches, we must pay attention, so that we know how to act for the future. With the current extreme drought where I live, I have had to put a halt to any wild plant harvesting. They simply cannot withstand that extractive impact. Instead, my efforts have gone into monitoring plants, gathering seeds, and broadcasting them where I can. And I spend more time tending to my container garden of herbs on my front porch. These changes throw off my ability to have fixed seasonal celebrations. Like the plants, the land, and the animals, witches are having to pay heed to these changes and adapt. It is heartbreaking to witness this struggle, but getting out into the land and paying attention teaches us and shows us the next steps we must take.

As you do this, choose your own path and know that it does not need to look like what others are doing. Observe, take part, notice, and integrate this knowledge. The spirits of the land will show you their own seasonal cycles.

Observing and documenting the annual cycles of the environment you inhabit can help you define your own seasonal patterns. This may take a year or more to complete, but it is well worth it. Just make note of all your observations during each month of the year. Start with the current month and move forward from there. Make notes of your activities, your feelings, and your observations of the land. Identify the fruits and edibles that are available to you.

For instance, here are my entries for August through November of this past year. Use them as an example of how to start your own seasonal calendar:

**August:** Busy, rushing, many social and work engagements. Huckleberries are ripe. Grasses are dry and land is in shades of beige. Tree fruits still ripening, may be available in September. Goldenrod blooming, yarrow, too. Elderberries ready to harvest in canyons. Daylight noticeably waning. Wildfire.

**September:** Busy, busy. Fruits are ripening rapidly, and the urge to go harvest is high—almost stressful. Gathering for winter stores. Land is golden, wheat crops golden, corn reaching maturity, last rounds of hay being made by farmers. Goldenrod still blooming and pearly everlasting, too. Some paintbrush flowers are blooming high up, yarrow persists. Wildfire and smoke haze.

**October:** Activities high, but feel that they will be slowing down in the following month. Winding down from fruit harvesting. Cooling air and lingering smoke from wildfire. Daylight very noticeably shorter. Gourds and winter squash available, more root vegetables. Food is heartier.

**November:** Slowing down, light waning. Winter squash season. Cool air nipping at the skin, frost some nights. Snow should come by mid-month. Dreams increasing, more sleep. Lots of ginger in the diet to warm the belly and body.

These observations continue through the rest of the year in much the same manner. I have included a practice at the end of this chapter that can help you build your own seasonal celebrations based on what the land and plants are doing in your location. Working with the description of your genius loci that you created in chapter 3 can be very helpful to you here as well.

## Daily Cycles

Just as each season of the year has significance in our lives, so do the days of the week. Each day of the week has a planetary ruler—a planet that governs it. You can use these rulers as energetic inspiration and support for certain points of focus and magic. However, you don't have to use them in any strict sense. When you do magic or are centering your day around an activity or ritual, it's nice to plan, but magic is also done because you have a need. Your practice needs to remain flexible and spontaneous. Don't let a false idea about perfect timing stop you from performing magic or ritual when you need or want to. Planetary rulers are here to inspire us and lend support and focus, but only if we choose to rely on them.

If planetary magic and veneration is something that interests you, it can be a great and gentle introduction to deity work. Just do work associated with that planet on that day. If, for example, I want to work with Venus, I simply do all workings and devotions with her on her day, which is Friday.

*Monday—Moon*

A wonderful day to perform magic of the home and hearth. The moon is connected to the element of Water, so this can be a great day to do the water-based magic of healing, cleansing, nurturing projects, and dreaming. The moon is associated with the sign of Cancer. White, blue, and silver are great colors to use on this day in your practice.

*Tuesday—Mars*

Mars is the god of war, passion, sex, defense, and attack. Mars' day can be helpful for starting projects with gusto, for laying down fierce protection (the kind that bites back), and for any workings where you need some extra "umph." Mars is ruled by the element of Fire and is strong, robust, and aggressive. The warrior planet is associated with the signs of Aries and Scorpio. Red, black, and orange are the colors of Mars.

*Wednesday—Mercury*

This is the perfect day for all things related to communications and technology, like sending texts, emails, messages, and so on. I feel that Wednesday is a rather all-purpose day, as it can help with the flow of commerce, communication, eloquence, and investigation. Mercury is ruled by the element of Air and is associated with the signs Gemini and Virgo. Yellow is the color of Mercury.

### Thursday—Jupiter

Jupiter is associated with all things fun, joyous, and expansive. This is a noble "kingly" planet, and Jupiter's day is a great day to do works of expansion, gain notoriety, perform money magic, and for gathering abundance. Jupiter is associated with the sign of Sagittarius. Purple, deep blue, and lapis are the colors of Jupiter.

### Friday—Venus

Friday is my favorite day of the week—not because it's the start of the weekend, but because it is ruled by Venus. Venus is traditionally about love, beauty, flirtation, and sex, but the planet is also about money and how we attract things to us. Aesthetics, the arts, fashion, and being seen are highlights here. It's a great day to do love and attraction magic. Venus finds herself in all elemental forms and rules the signs of Libra and Taurus. Green, pink, red, and copper are the colors of Venus.

## Saturday—Saturn

Saturn is associated with old Father Time. This is a great day for building structures and discipline. Saturn is often maligned in astrology and seen as quite an oppressive and negative force, which can be true. But Saturn is also the positive "father" archetype of building structures that support us. Saturn's day is also a day for magics of binding, cursing, and banishing. (Mars is more amenable to attack.) This is a good day to do clearing magic. Saturn is associated with the metal lead and the color black.

## Sunday—Sun

As its name indicates, this is the day of the sun. This is one of those all-purpose days when anything goes. This day is great for the magics of vitality, health, money, being seen, blessing, and just generally great vibes. Personally, I find this a great day to do works of cleansing and blessing for the coming week, and to do some home cleaning and setting of protections. The sun rules Leo and is associated with gold and yellow.

## Lunar Cycles

For the longest time, I did not have the greatest relationship to the moon. It wasn't that I disliked the moon; it was just that I felt indifferent. I recognized her beauty and luminosity in the skies as she shifted through her phases, but I didn't feel much of a connection. I am a solar person and I felt more connected to the energies of the sun. If you identify as a witch, most people automatically assume that you're obsessed with the moon and have some powerful connection there. This may be true for some, but it wasn't for me.

With time, however, I discovered that I was able to track my magic, my projects, and my activities through the lunar cycles and live more attuned to them and how they were reflected in my life. I was also able to utilize them to track my menstrual cycles, which I found deeply connective and valuable in my practice. The moon taught me when to slow down and when to take advantage of the heightening of my power, which can vary wildly from person to person. If you're a person who bleeds monthly, this can be a valuable means of tracking and connection.

The moon is complicated, mysterious, and shifty. From an astrological perspective, the moon represents the home, the mother, and water, as well as how we nurture and receive nurturing and how we emote and connect with others emotionally. In tarot, the moon represents the unknown fears that we carry and what lies on the other side should we choose to explore it. The moon speaks to psychic connection and activity as well. When the moon moves through its phases, you may notice times when you are more "on" and others when you are more "off." Our energy waxes and wanes just like the moon.

The moon is one of the planetary bodies that significantly and personally impact us each day. The magnetic pull of the moon on the waters of our planet, on our bodies, and on the bodies of all living beings on this earth controls the cycles of our lives. The element of Water is associated with our hearts, emotions, and dreams, and can teach us much about these when we choose to work with it.

Observing the phases of the moon can be a very informative and magical act. I highly recommend using an app to track lunar phases and record them in your journal. Much of the time, we can see our own rhythms syncing up with the moon. If you want to add an extra layer of association, find a good astrology app that can show you what sign the moon is in. This can be very revealing, and you'll definitely notice those energetic patterns in the world around you.

When the moon is waxing, it means its light is increasing. This is a great time to do magics of increase, attraction, and gain. When waning, the moon's light is decreasing. This is a good time to do magics of decrease, repelling, and banishing. But remember: Do magic when it is necessary for you! If your car breaks down, you don't wait for the stars to align to get it fixed. You do it as soon as possible.

## Dark Moon

When the moon is completely dark, it means that it is close to the sun and in full shadow. Some suggest that this is the time to perform magical work. But I personally feel this is inaccurate. This is an excellent time for shadow work and for working with *spirit*. To me, this is when the moon becomes our deepest and most powerful ally, as it is not touched by the sun (at least to the naked eye). This is when the door opens for all creatures and beings of the night and of the liminal spaces to roam. At this time, spirit moves more freely, and you can connect more deeply with spirit within yourself. It is also when starlight is most visible, and when we can move through the shadows and darkness undetected.

When the moon is dark, take this opportunity to clean up your altar space and home in preparation for the new moon. It's a wonderful time to review journal entries, reflect on dreams, and ask guidance from the spirits, as they are very active (in my personal experience). You can also begin to reflect on the projects on which you want to focus for the upcoming new moon. And it's a wonderful time to do any cleansing, banishing, and releasing work, so think about things you want to finish. This is the time to take a moment for reflection, to slow down and rest.

### New Moon and Waxing Moon

This moon phase marks the beginning a new lunation cycle. It's the start of a new lunar month, and as such is the perfect time to begin something new. New-moon energy is my favorite, as I like to work this into my goals and plans for that cycle. Whatever intentions you set for that cycle you can watch grow or become more illuminated as the moon approaches fullness. It can be a fantastic way to track basically anything and do some planning for projects moving forward. This is where you can begin to blur the lines between the magical and the mundane. If you feel that's been something of a challenge for you, this is a wonderful place to start.

I feel that this is also a good time to give monthly offerings to spirits and to start things off afresh on a good footing. Lay fresh flowers on your altar, fill up glasses with water for spirits, light some incense, and enjoy the fresh new energy.

### Full Moon

This phase marks the peak of the moon's energy. At this time, the sun is opposing the moon and illuminates it fully. This is a powerfully energetic time to really start something off with a bang. Full-moon energy can be electric and erratic, as the full amplification of light cascades down upon us here on earth. As you may notice, sometimes things get a little odd around a full moon.

In the days leading up to a full moon, I like to perform magics of gain, attraction, and increase, because I can tap into the increasing power of the moon's phase. This is also a good time to "charge" items of power and other objects. My final day of magic focuses on the night of the full moon itself, so that explosion of power really sets it off!

You can make moon water during this time as well. Take some clean water (tap or spring water works well), place a stone in it (hag stones, quartz, or a piece of silver), and allow this combination to sit in the moonlight for a few hours. If you want to preserve your moon water, add a bit of Everclear to it. One friend of mine wraps his bottle of moon water in a cloth so that no rays of sunlight can touch it. I find this a helpful way to keep it charged.

## Seasonal Cycles

Seasonal cycles can be celebrated along with the moon phases. If you wish, you can create your own seasonal celebrations, defined by your relationship to the land on which you live. Equinoxes and solstices are phenomena we all experience, as they can be tracked by the motion of the earth in relation to the sun, so that is a good place to start.

*Winter and the Winter Solstice*

The shortest day and longest night of the year occur on the winter solstice. This is when you are shrouded in the depths of darkness. However, joy and hope of the sun's return comes the following day, when the light begins to increase ever so slightly each day.

In winter, you may find yourself indoors more often, keeping warm and eating heartier foods. Most plant life is dormant now. You may find yourself working on handiwork and crafts of the home—making repairs, moving forward on projects, doing more home cooking, and nurturing ideas of what may come when spring arrives. You may also slow down a bit during this time. Some other aspects of your life may speed up, however, as there are many cultural celebrations around this time. You may take advantage of deeper and longer sleep cycles, as it's an invitation to amalgamate and metabolize what you have gathered and experienced in the warmer months. This is the deepening of dreamtime that you enter when fall has come and passed. Magical workings and rituals of this time of year may be inclined toward bringing light and life into the home.

Some "deck the halls" at this time of year, bringing in branches of conifers to decorate the house. These branches also have a magical use. Pine and fir can be burned during the winter to cleanse a space of negativity and bad spirits, and they also serve this same purpose when hung around the home. Decorating altars with evergreens and bright candles is a lovely way to keep your connection with the land moving and active. Because some feel that this is a "dead" time of year when it comes to plant life, you may reach for these evergreens—still green and full of life—to remind yourself that you are also moving and full of life, even in the dead of winter.

Winter walks along the land can be useful, even if plant life is dormant. You can learn to identify and be in witness to your plant allies and land kin through all their life phases, even when they're shrouded in snow or appear lifeless. A favorite pastime of mine during winter is to find the bones of plants that have died back—stalks and seeds and the remaining bits of plant life. Learning to recognize them in this phase can be useful and may help you discover new stands of plants. You can also learn to identify trees by bark and twig— it's challenging, but fun!

Winter is also a beautiful time to reflect on the coming year and to set goals. In some ways, the time after the solstice can be looked on as a time of new-moon energy, as the sun is revived after declining in light ever since the summer solstice. Generating ideas, dreaming, and scheming are good uses of your time during this season. You can see your ideas come to life in the spring and into fruition in summer.

Connecting with ancestors and spirits continues during this time of year, as the veil between worlds remains a bit thin but increases as the light increases. It's a great time for dreamwork, as you are invited to rest deeply in this season. Trance work and journeying are also potent at this time.

Traditional winter celebrations are winter solstice, or Yule, celebrated from December 21st to January 1st, and Imbolc, celebrated around February 1st, heralding the beginning of spring. Imbolc also marks a liminal space between winter and spring. It's still wintery, but life begins to move during this time.

### Spring

Finally, the light begins to quicken, the days grow longer, and you can begin to see the stirring of spring sometime in February. Depending on where you live, you may notice that the buds are beginning to grow a little more—a small reminder that the fullness of spring is well on its way. Bear magic is particularly potent to me in the early spring months, as bears begin to awaken from their dreamtime hibernation and move about in the world again, seeking out greens and roots to nourish their bodies. I appreciate the cycles bears hold with the land, as they teach us how and when to rest, when to emerge into the world, and when to collect nourishment for the cooler seasons.

As the light increases and the soil warms, greens begin to grow, inviting us to bring green and vibrant foods back into our diets and to stimulate digestion. Dandelion, cleavers, chickweed, nettle, and violets get our digestion moving and can help stimulate the lymphatic system, which may have gone stagnant over the winter months. Some of these plants, being bitters, awaken our taste buds after a season of rich and fatty foods. They help us to move and digest in preparation for the coming season of more greens and, often, a dietary shift. Spiritually speaking, this is a good time to develop relationships to these seemingly simple but powerful plant allies. Discover new stands of nettle and find a patch of cleavers or chickweed in damp and rich soils. Begin to explore a little more as life springs up around you. As the sap in trees and plants begins to move, so do we experience our own sap rising and moving. A life force reenters the body, enabling us to move and create with gusto.

Spring is a beautiful time to set into motion those dreams and ideas that you pondered during the winter months. Now you can plant seeds and nurture them, so that you may see them to fruition. Offerings of milk, cream, butter, and honey are welcome during this time by plants, trees, and land allies. It's a great time to perform the magics of generating abundance and starting projects off on the right foot. This time can be looked on as waxing quarter-moon energy. It's growing into fullness.

A spring cleaning may be in order for altar spaces, herb cabinets, gardens, and any spaces where you keep your magical items. It's time to freshen them up for the coming busy months of late spring and summer.

The garden may become a focal point for some, as it's time to make decisions on who you'll plant and nurture and bring into your life. As you begin to move outdoors more, this can be a great time to freshen up protective wards around the home and outside of it. For example, placing charged and marked stones at the four corners of your home or property can be both grounding and protective for the space in which you live. Decorate spaces with spring flower arrangements—a reflection of what is happening in the outer world happening in your internal world, which the altar often represents.

Traditional spring celebrations include Imbolc and Beltane, which is seen by some as the start of summer. Beltane, or Walpurgis Night, can be viewed as being opposite in a way to Samhain, or Halloween. It is a night of ecstasy, fire rites, and fertility. Hawthorn, a Fire tree, is often associated with this day. Hawthorn blooms smell of sex, or semen, and the wood burns bright and hot. Hawthorn is connected to the *fae*, or fairies, who are fiercely protective of trees. They also mark the hedge between worlds and are often seen as the darling tree of the green witch's world. Hawthorn blossoms and needles collected on Beltane day are a powerful addition to a witch's herb collection.

### Summer

The light and sun begin to reach their apex, and then go into decline after the summer solstice. Summer, depending on where you live, can be a time that is full of life, or one that heralds yet another dormant cycle during which you find yourself indoors a little more, escaping from the heat of the long days and nourishing your body with water-rich, cooling foods. At this time, you may be at the peak of your activities, rushing around, tending to all those seeds you dreamed of during the winter, planted in the spring, and have tended as the months grew warmer. You're partaking of the products of your labor, eating more fresh fruits and vegetables from your garden or a local farm. You may even find yourself gathering wild foods like berries, edible plants and roots, and fruit from trees. Plant medicine is also in high gear, as many medicinal plants reach their peak in this growing season.

Summer can be seen as full-moon energy, so it can be a time of erratic swings. Sometimes in those high days of summer, my nerves can feel a bit frayed. Festivals and parties abound, and folks move about more freely in the warming weather. Not everyone is enthusiastic about summer heat and celebrations, however, as it can feel like a winter of sorts for winter-loving people. Those who live in the low desert can experience extreme heat at this time and often withdraw to the coolness under trees and within their homes. For more northern folks, this can be a great time for medicinal plant harvesting and for frolicking about in woods and fields.

Saint John's wort is chief among the summer plants, as it is liquid sun when infused in alcohol or oil, turning a bright shade of red, mimicking the redness you see behind your closed eyelids when you turn your face toward the sun. This plant can be a valuable medicine in the depths of winter because of its potential use to treat depression. Saint John's wort harvested on the summer solstice can be an important herb in the witch's plant-ally arsenal.

You may be invited to slow down and revel in the accessibility you have to the land during this time. Bathing in rivers and springs, and seeking water sources for cooling nourishment are a wonderful way to connect to the Water element during a hot, fiery season. Appreciating the contrasts around you during this time can be valuable. Seeking the coolness under trees and connecting with your tree kin is also easier in high summer, as you're more able to identify your plant and tree friends.

Summer rites and rituals include celebrating the gathering of abundance. The solstice proper is a particularly propitious time to gather magical and medicinal herbs from gardens and wild spaces. Some of these plants include yarrow, elder, vervain, chamomile, mugwort, burdock, thyme, calendula, and, of course, Saint John's wort.

The summer solstice occurs when the sun enters the sign of Cancer, around June 20th to June 22nd. Lammas, traditionally seen as the end of summer, falls on August 1st and marks the first harvest and a noticeable decrease in daylight hours. It also marks the descent into the darkness of our next season, fall.

### Fall

Mabon, Harvest Home, or simply the autumn equinox, falls around September 21st and marks the beginning of fall. As in the spring, the days and nights are more equal in length in the fall. It is perhaps considered the most witchy of the seasons, because the nights grow longer and spirits move with more potency and frequency. There is often a lovely, warm and cozy energy in the air, as the leaves begin to turn, winter squash becomes available, and all the regalia of the coming Samhain and Halloween season begins to appear. Some begin to decorate and prepare their homes to call in this season of the witch. But truth be told, it is always the season of the witch. We persist through all seasons.

In fall, you can find cooling nights, with brightly glowing orange-and-red harvest moons hanging low on the gloaming horizon. There is something truly magical about this time that calls to us deeply within our spirits. Warm spiced drinks may become more frequent, along with well-spiced foods that warm us for the coming of winter.

Much lore surrounds this potent season. You can sense the stirring and rising of the witch gods and goddesses as they awaken from the earth and move into your dreams and trance states. You begin the journey into the Otherworld and to the realm of the ancestors. Working with your beloved dead during this time can be quite potent, as the veil grows thinner as you get closer to Samhain. Erecting an ancestor altar can be an excellent project for this time of year. Arranging photos of your beloved dead on an altar set specifically for them—with a bowl of water, a white candle, their favorite foods, and heartfelt prayers—is a simple way to connect with your ancestors.

Psychopomps, gods, and goddesses who are known to traverse between worlds are also easier to connect with during this time. I find that specifically Hekate and Hermes are much easier to work with in the waning and liminal space of autumn.

Herbs that you gathered in spring and summer become helpful here as they begin to fade underground for the season. However, you may find late-blooming flowers like yarrow, goldenrod, and rabbitbrush, and hawthorn and elderberries may still persist. Other fruits, like apples and pears, can be found as well and make a fine offering on the altar and for creating delicious baked goods to offer to friends, family, and your beloved dead. Nuts are also available, as are the magical woods of hazel and oak, which offer up their fruits for the altar as well.

This time of year has waning-moon energy, a slowing down as you begin to approach winter. During this time, you gather and harvest much for the coming season of darkness, when you'll huddle up in your home, cultivating dreams and deeper connections to the spirits.

Fall includes the holidays of the fall equinox, and that most famous of witches' holidays, Samhain, which is also seen as the witches' New Year. I find this to be a particularly good time for divining about the year ahead, taking stock of your spiritual development and where your efforts might best be placed. Divinations on the night of Samhain are an excellent use of your ritual time, especially if you're not the type to engage in popular Halloween revelries.

There is no wrong or right way to celebrate the seasonal cycles of the land on which you live. Pay attention, and you'll find that the land will lead you in a direction that works for you and your relationship to place.

### Practice: Defining Your Wheel of the Year
You can begin to define your own wheel of the year by observing and documenting the annual cycles of

the environment you inhabit. Start by answering these questions to establish the pattern of the seasonal cycles for your locale:

- When does spring usually arrive, and what marks its arrival for you?

- When does the summer growing cycle begin and end, and what flourishes then?

- When does the harvest season begin, and what marks that transition for you?

- When does winter begin and what changes mark its arrival?

Then begin to record what you see around you for each month of the year, starting with the current month and moving forward from there. Here are examples of questions you can ask:

- When does the sun rise? When does it set? Are there changes in the light?

- Are the temperatures warm? Cold? Moderate? Changing?

- Is it rainy? Dry? Windy? Calm? Are there any unusal conditions prevailing? Fire? Smoke? Flooding? Drought?

- What fruits, berries, and edibles are available?

- What flowers are in bloom? What grasses? Which mosses?

- What colors dominate the landscape?

- Are the trees budding? In full leaf? In transition? Bare?

- What animals are in evidence around you? Are they mating? Hibernating?

- What bird songs do you hear?

- What insects do you see?

- What activities are you pursuing? Are your personal habits adjusting to any seasonal changes?

- What emotions or feelings are you experiencing?

- Has climate change affected your environment in perceptible ways?

Use this list to get started, then add your own observations. This practice will take a year to complete, but it will be well worth it.

# Chapter 6

# Ancestors and Descendants

*The songs of our ancestors are also the songs of our children.*
—Philip Carr-Gomm

Our ancestors were born of the earth. They lived out their lives connected to the earth—to a culture, to traditions, to a place. And, in death, they returned to the earth. Thus, as earth witches, it is particularly important for us to reach out to the spirits of those who have gone before us—both those to whom we are related by blood and those to whom we are related by lineage. By maintaining these ancestral ties, we connect to powerful spiritual forces rooted deep in our conscious and unconscious selves. We open ourselves to receiving messages from both the world we inhabit and the world in which our ancestors lived. And by doing so, we ground ourselves more firmly in the earth itself. For we, too, are born of the earth. We live out our lives rooted in the land we inhabit, but also rooted in spirit by our ancestors. They lead us, watch out for us, and teach us. And, like them, we shall also return to the earth in the fullness of time.

As I write this, the air is cooling, the fall equinox draws near, the sun is waning, and I can feel the ancestors becoming livelier. I'm gazing upon a burgundy picture frame that houses a photograph of my late Mamaw in her nightgown that sits on my large altar, which also serves as a writing desk. I imagine the smell of her perfume and remember her fondly in her yellow-and-blue kitchen decorated everywhere with ceramic chickens and roosters. I remember her azalea-colored lipsticks and the many scarves that she wore that I inherited when she passed. They now decorate my home, serving as altar cloths. I wear some in remembrance of her.

As the days grow shorter into the darkening of the year, the ancestors become more alive and present in our lives. While any time is a good time to work with your ancestors, this is a particularly potent time in which to do so. I share my morning coffee with my Mamaw; I chat with her and offer her sweets. And in return, I know she's looking out for me. I know that she urges along my spells and sees to it that what I need travels to me. I know I have other ancestors, known and unknown to me, doing this work as well.

Because I grew up in a military family that moved every two and a half years, I had little time to forge deep bonds. And when I did, I found myself once again on the move. This nomadic existence continued into my adult life, and I now live on the farthest coast from my southern relatives. This separation created problems for me when I began to explore my ancestors. You see, on one side of my family, it was traditional to bury the dead, to leave no markers, and to forget them. There is no record of their existence, no family elders to tell stories. So I have large gaps in my family tree. Unknown fathers, mothers who died in childbirth, broken familial lines. I am but one of many who have a broken and confusing ancestry, and it is difficult to put the pieces back together again. Despite these challenges, however, I have learned that you can connect with your ancestors, both those known and those unknown to you. In this chapter, we will explore this necessary work.

## The Beloved Dead

Working with your ancestors is very much like dealing with the living—some you invite in, some you don't. Deciding which ones you will work with is, in my opinion, up to you. You do not need to deal with them all. Frankly, many of my ancestors ticked me off or made me uncomfortable, and I didn't know how to work with them in a tangible and practical way. Over the years, however, I have softened, and now they're an integral part of my practice.

Through research, dreams, and other experiences, I have come to understand that I had some ancestors who didn't take too kindly to my witchcraft. I come from a line of pastors and ministers of deeply Christian faith, so my heretical ways weren't very welcomed. When engaging in dreamwork, I've even had a few male ancestors literally shake me into wakefulness while I was reaching that blessed point in my dream where I was about to receive an answer. They bothered me and I shooed them away, knowing that they did not support my cause. This left me fraught with odd, uncomfortable feelings and a recognition that not all my ancestors wore halos. However, I have discovered through my work that I have many amazing and supportive ancestors as well. It just took time, patience, and practice to get in touch with them.

Getting to know your beloved dead begins with boundaries. It's likely that you may not have bonds with some familiar ancestors due to trauma, abuse, abandonment, neglect, or other circumstances. And you may have very tight bonds with others, like those who raised you with gentle and loving hands, taught you, and supported you. You *do* get to choose with whom you bond, however. I believe that blood is not always thicker than water; we always have a choice. It is good, nonetheless, to hold those ancestors with whom you may not agree with compassion. They were once human, and humans do screw up. I have forgiven many of my less-savory ancestors for their trespasses against me and others in my family, but it was a great challenge and took a lot of effort. I let go of those feelings so that I could move on in life with more peace of mind.

Processing and healing intergenerational trauma requires a lifetime of work. When we engage with our ancestors and heal these broken parts, we are doing the work of ancestral healing, which we pass on to future generations. How this looks for you may be very different from anyone else's ancestor work.

Because I have large gaps in my historical family lines, I felt called to take a DNA test to better understand my place of origin and who my ancestors may have been—where they came from and where they may have migrated. I found it to be very helpful, because there was simply no way for me to know where parts of my family had originated. This test allowed me to orient my witchcraft practices to some of the influences of the lands from which my ancestors originally hailed. I was able to weave Scottish, Scandinavian, and German lore and folk magic into my own spiritual practice, which helped generate a sense of rootedness where before I had so often felt lost.

In Western society, our ancestors are largely forgotten or ignored, because this society has a deep fear of death, the dying, and those who have passed beyond. As earth witches, however, we know that we stand on the bones of those who came before us. Their blood runs through our veins. Most of them want to see us do well and are invested in our well-being and success in life. Ancestor work is a great entryway for spirit work, as our ancestors are safe, benevolent, and generally easy to access because they are always with us.

Branching out into ancestor work may seem strange or intimidating for some of you reading this, but let me assure you that it will be worth it. My beloved dead have saved me on more than one occasion, through dream omens, in waking life, and more. They can be your first line of spiritual defense when you get into tight situations or are dealing with spirits who do not have your best interests at heart. Cultivating and forging bonds with your beloved dead is not just worthwhile, it is an honorable act that heals you and deepens your practice.

## Discovering Your Origins

Many of us come from broken lineages or don't even know who our parents and family are, which creates some difficulty in understanding our origins. If you're able, start by asking questions of family members, blood relations or otherwise. Someone in your family has probably done the ancestral bookkeeping. After asking around, I was able to find a whole stack of genealogical research that a great aunt had done for my family. Yet I still know only one line of my family's history. And, unfortunately, it is a branch of my family to which I have not felt very connected. However, this research provided me with information about where I came from, and what that part of the family had to endure as they migrated and became integrated into the New World.

Aunts, uncles, grandparents, and other family members can be powerful resources if you have access to them. They are a great place to start uncovering your origins. Simply engaging in conversation about your family's origins can be connective and revealing. Ask about what particular ancestors liked, what their passions were, and what their favorite foods were. These tidbits can inform your ancestor work and supply you with important information about how best to proceed with certain ancestors.

DNA tests can be particularly useful here, but they often leave us with more questions than answers. For example, I discovered that I have Coptic Egyptian heritage. Who knew! What I have found helpful about DNA testing is that it gave me a point of cultural focus within my studies of the Craft and helped direct and orient my spiritual practice. Often, we feel quite displaced as family lines blur or are scattered to the winds. DNA testing can help you learn where to orient your practices as a witch and bring you to a better understanding of your origins so you can focus your folkloric and cultural studies within your craft. When I discovered my early Pennsylvania Dutch ancestry, I was able to study their rich and amazing folk-magic traditions. I have now integrated this heritage into my practice with a comfortable sense of familiarity. Be open and call your ancestors in. You don't need to know exactly where you came from to be connected to them; it is in your blood. Your ancestors are always with you, often waiting for you to notice them.

It is important to note that not all your ancestors are related by blood. Many folks come from adopted families or have a chosen family—I know I do. These people are also your ancestors by bond and love, and they deserve as much honor as your blood ancestors. Please include them. You also have ancestors by lineage, those who may have passed on spiritual and religious traditions, ancestral skills, a craft or trade. These ancestors should also be honored by you. If you're a basket weaver or someone who creates textiles, you were taught by someone who was taught by someone else, who, in turn, was taught by another. And this line becomes the lineage of craftspeople to whom you are connected. The information and art of your craft was passed down from generation to generation, and just because you are not related by blood to these folks doesn't mean you can't honor them. Weave them into your veneration and honor them through your practice. It may just help you heal some severed or broken ties.

## Ancestral Altars

Setting up an ancestral altar is rather easy. Just adorn a small table with white and light-blue fabrics and place any photographs of your beloved dead on the altar, along with white or light-blue candles to light as needed. These color combinations bring in a calm, peaceful, and cooling influence. Keep a dedicated glass for water and a dish for incense on the altar as well. The water acts as a conduit for contact and refreshment for your beloved dead, while the incense offers them a source of sustenance and lifts up your prayers to them. Candles provide warmth and yet another point of contact, as they light the way for your ancestors to find you.

If you're able, use a water glass, spoon, or a dish that once belonged to that ancestor to strengthen the ancestral connection, or perhaps objects your ancestors once used on their own altars. To these personal items, add dishes of food and other offerings. These needn't be big; just small ones will suffice. You can place trinkets and objects that may have been important to your ancestors on the altar as well. Say an ancestor was a carpenter, for example. You can put woodworking tools or beautiful wooden objects on your altar. If your ancestor was a great cook, place a beautiful bowl or mixing dish on the altar as an offering. My Mamaw was fond of chickens and roosters and the colors blue and yellow, so I always make sure to include these themes around her photograph. I'm sure you get the idea.

While it's nice to have an altar dedicated solely to your ancestors, you don't always need to erect a full altar. Space can be limited in many homes and pesky but beloved pets may like to investigate these curious locations. Shelves and desks also make great ancestral altars, because you can place your ancestors' photos there, along with a glass of water and a dish for serving foods. If you burn candles, be sure that there is nothing combustible above the candle's flame, like another shelf or a window curtain. I keep my grandmothers in the place I frequent most, my writing desk and main altar. I like to keep them close as I do my work.

If you are going to keep an ancestor altar, you must understand a few key things. First, don't set it up in your bedroom. This is widely seen as taboo when it comes to ancestor work because it is disrespectful. I know I wouldn't want to be dressing and undressing in front of my Mamaw, and I definitely wouldn't want her to see me engaged in other bedroom activities. Ancestors can sometimes visit at inopportune times. While you do want to forge a connection to them, you don't need them knocking on the door at all hours. Keeping their altars in a bedroom invites them to be in contact during both sleeping and relaxing hours. Boundaries are important here to keep this sort of contact under control. You can, however, invite ancestors to engage in dreamwork with you, via your bedside dreamwork altar if you have one (see chapter 7). I do this only under specific conditions when I want to connect with them via dreams.

Another taboo is salt, which I have seen used across various traditions and cultures. Salt acts as a spirit repellant and can drive your ancestors away if kept on or near your ancestral altar. Minimize the use of *very* salty foods as well. This may not upset your ancestors, but it may inhibit contact with them if you keep them on or near the altar. Foods that contain some salt don't seem to be a problem, but don't keep a dish of pure salt right on the altar.

It is also advisable not to place pictures of the living on your ancestral altar, as this is thought to bring them a speedy death. Keep those pictures in another space.

## Ancestral Offerings

Ancestral offerings are quite simple to make and can range widely in type. Liquid offerings can be drinks like tea, coffee (a favorite), water, wine, juices, or anything you imagine may be refreshing. Be sure to consider the effects that the drink may have on you, because it will have the same effect on your ancestors as well. Is it energizing or relaxing? If you need them active and lively, coffee and tea are good choices. Having a cozy moment? Maybe some chamomile tea would be nice. Consider the person's favorite drinks and offer those with a few words. Then leave the offering for a day or two. Just be sure to remove the drinks before they spoil. It's just bad manners to leave old and moldy drinks on your ancestral altar, and it also attracts negative and unclean energy. And avoid anything that may have been a problem for them, like alcohol or cigarettes. My grandmother died from smoking cigarettes and, as much as I know she might like one, I do not offer them to her.

Food offerings can be very simple. I like to buy special treats for my ancestors—especially sweets, as many in my family have a sweet tooth. Sometimes, as I walk through the grocery store, I am pulled to some lemon doughnuts or a chocolate cake and get a funny feeling that my ancestors might like it. (Of course, it could also just be my own sweet tooth talking.) Baking sweet treats for your ancestors is another great way to honor them. Does your family have a special recipe that has been passed down from generation to generation? Working with these familial foods is an amazing way to honor your ancestors in a special, time-giving way.

Bread is a food offering that everyone loves. If you're partial to baking, try baking a loaf and leaving it on the altar along with some butter. Bread was often a staple in ancestral diets. Baking bread also carries with it a magical and alchemical aspect. If you're not much of a cook, just try following a recipe. The act of learning and going through the motions of making food is also an act of ancestral devotion and honor.

Your offerings need not be limited to sweet treats, however, as savory foods are welcome as well. I like to offer a portion of my dinner to my ancestors on a dish dedicated just to them, even if it's just takeout. You don't have to offer them a full meal; a few bites will work. Again, think of recipes that your family may have cooked or a favorite meal an ancestor may have liked. Such offerings can be a wonderful way to reach out to them, as cooking and sharing meals is a deeply connective act.

You don't need to bury the remains of your offerings. To dispose of them, just toss them into the trash or compost. As a friend of mine says, it would be weird if you invited your Aunt Jane over for dinner and then buried her leftovers in the backyard. You can leave a particularly special offering at a crossroads, but avoid throwing food items in rivers or running water because it can (and does) disrupt the fragile ecology of these waterways. Trash and compost are just fine.

While food and drink are staple offerings, you needn't be limited to just these two sources of nourishment and connection to your beloved dead. Another fabulous way to make an offering is through scent. Did your ancestors have a favorite perfume or fragrance? Maybe you can buy a bottle and leave it on their altar. My Mamaw was particularly fond of bright magenta lipsticks and body powders. Leaving these items as gifts can also count as an offering. Spritz some perfume or open a container of cosmetics for them to enjoy. You're really only limited by your imagination here. Tune in and ask them what they want to receive, noting any physical sensations, smells, or tastes they communicate to you through your bodily senses. Be creative and free with your offerings. Your ancestors will be pleased and pleasantly surprised when you leave them gifts, just as they would have been when they were living.

Performing devotional acts like knitting, gardening, hunting, or any task that an ancestor enjoyed is another form of offering. Make that weeding, spinning, or any activity that you engage in a devotional and sacred act to honor your ancestors. They will connect with you through these repetitive movements and, in these spaces, you can often shift into a meditative state that allows for the transmission of communication between you and your beloved dead.

## Problematic Ancestors

I like to think that our ancestors know, once they have crossed over, in what ways they may have been problematic in living their lives. Many of our ancestors may have been violent colonizers or slave owners, or may have committed grievous crimes, abused people, and so on. It is my feeling that, when these people move on to the other side, they realize how these behaviors were problematic and they transcend or ascend from them. *This does not absolve them from those actions, however.*

So how do you work with ancestors who may have contributed to destructive and oppressive ways of being? Ask them how they would like to make amends, through your simple prayers and your contact with them. See what they say. These amends can then be lived through you and your actions as you move through the world. Ancestor work is ultimately healing work, and while you cannot completely heal those who may have suffered through past actions, you can take steps in your own life to reset the course in the right direction. This may include making reparations, voting, and supporting infrastructure that aids those who still suffer under oppression. It may mean volunteering or donating your money and time to good causes and mutual-aid efforts. You can also turn inward and confront your own problematic behaviors and correct them.

These amends become a living tribute that corrects the course of history and redirects the future. And you can pass this healing on to coming generations to teach them how to give selflessly and to practice love and care for others, rather than just tolerating them.

## Paying It Forward

When I was about eleven years old, I recall rushing to the mailbox one day to find a box that my grandmother had sent me. When I ripped it open, I was surprised to see copies of the two-part documentary *The Private Life of Plants*. Curious, I played the program and a miraculous thing happened. I watched as plants, in sped-up motion, breathed and exhaled with the sun and shade of the trees above them. They moved and breathed just as we do. They reached for the sun and creeped and crawled to their growing destinations. They had clever ways of dispersing seeds and sharing and extracting resources from their environment. They knew where to grow and where not to grow. They knew how to thrive and survive. The infectious enthusiasm of the narrator, David Attenborough, had a profound impact on me.

After watching the documentary, I stepped outside very carefully and looked around me. I felt millions of eyes upon me—the eyes of my plant kin. I felt as if I now knew their secrets and I saw them as sentient, feeling, breathing beings. My whole world was forever changed. Little did my grandmother know (or maybe she did) that she had instilled within me a recognition of animism in the world. What I had previously been taught was lifeless matter was suddenly and brilliantly alive.

A decade and a half later, my grandmother passed away. One of my greatest regrets is that I did not spend much time with her as a young adult. Now that I'm older, I've seen the error of not honoring and giving selflessly of my time to my elders—those I knew would become my ancestors.

Someday, we, too, will become ancestors to those who come after us. Reflecting on our own mortality can be a disturbing but necessary thing. But we will all die, and it is thoughtful to consider what you may leave behind for those who come after you. When I dwell on this, I think about my grandmothers and what they shared with me while I was growing up. They instilled in me a love of nature and of cooking meals to share with others, not to mention the other valuable skills they taught me—even the small and seemingly minute things that they shared with me. Like when to apply body powder after a shower and where. How to apply lipstick. How and where to place a hummingbird feeder. How to cook polenta. All these little things they passed on to me, and I, too, will pass them on to someone else. All these things are part of familial legacy and traditions passed on from one generation to the next. How do you want to be remembered? What skills and tricks do you have to share with others?

Paying careful attention to children within family bonds, including nieces and nephews or even chosen family kin, is particularly important. As a person with no children and who doesn't plan to have any, I pay close attention to those youths in my life and I share with them what I know, like how to identify plants, how a plant can be useful, or what a plant's medicine is. Offering up books and videos like the nature documentary my grandmother sent and the *National Geographic* subscription she paid for helps orient their minds in thoughtful ways. These little things had great impact on me growing up and well into my adult life, and I plan to pass that precious information on to those I love.

In our culture, which constantly promotes rugged individualism and alienation, we must counteract this focus by getting involved with our kin and community. It's there that we can pass on precious knowledge and change the lives of others. Through even the simplest of acts, we can forge connections and pass on our legacy of knowledge and perspective. Not only will this greatly impact others, it can also save a life by shifting it toward something that brings the person impacted back to the earth. If you have knowledge, give of it freely to those you love and share it with those who will listen. When you, too, become an ancestor—and eventually you will—rest assured that you will be taken care of and thought of in the afterlife, especially if you share the gift of ancestor veneration with another.

*Practice: Calling Your Ancestors*

A simple way to call in your ancestors is through prayer, in the morning or evening. Prayer does not need to be complicated. Just speak from your heart. Express your needs and desires, and what you're currently holding within yourself. Don't worry if this conversation feels one-sided. Trust me when I say they are listening.

A prayer can be as simple as this:

*I call to you, my ancestors known and unknown to me. I call to my ancestors benevolent to me and my cause, and I ask that you hear my prayer and be with me now.*

Tell your ancestors where you have been struggling and what you have been dealing with in your life. Chat with them as you would if they were still alive. Tell them you remember them, and that you reflect upon the fond memories you still carry.

Invite your ancestors to contact you. Ask for very specific signs to show up throughout your day or in your dreams. For example, if butterflies were particularly special to an ancestor, ask for a sign in the form of butterflies. You can use anything that may have attracted them—the more specific you are, the less vague the answer will be. When you begin to engage in ancestor work, spiritual activity around you will pick up rather quickly. You'll begin to have dreams that are stronger and have more meaning. You may even notice more synchronistic events playing out in your life.

If your ancestors were tied to any religious or spiritual traditions, you can also pray to them within that tradition. The act of praying in the same way that they did serves to strengthen and deepen your connection if you are comfortable with it. Did your family have a traditional prayer or method of praying? Give it a try and see how effective it can be.

You do not need a particular physical setting to pray. Find a quiet space, perhaps light a white candle or set out a glass of water and some incense, and pray from the heart. Take a moment to breathe deeply and see what you feel. Ancestors will often move through feelings within your body. Notice if you have any cravings for foods that you might not crave otherwise, as this can be a food-offering indicator. Notice your sense of smell, as your ancestors can communicate with you in this way as well.

*Practice: Ancestor Meditation*

Meditation practices can also help you connect with your ancestors. In this meditation, ask for messages from them and then listen to what arises. You needn't be hearing them with your physical ears; they may come through to your inner ear—the one connected to spirit and all life.

If you find this work difficult or are confused by it, try listening to more than just your human kin. Do you communicate with plants or stones easily? Doing so can help bridge the gap of listening deeply and understanding any messages that come through from your ancestors. If you have difficulty listening deeply, a meditation practice can help to quiet the noise in your head. Pay attention to sight, sound, physical feelings, and smell while in prayer and communion with your ancestors. Don't overthink it. When finished, write what you experienced in your journal and see if you can pick up any threads of connection.

# Chapter 7

# The Dreamworld

*Dreaming is the main function of the mind.*
—don Miguel Ruiz

Some shamanic traditions teach that our entire universe was born from a dream. If this is true, then the dreamworld can be cultivated as a realm in which we connect with both land and spirits. And learning to navigate and understand the dreamworld can be one of the most important practices for earth witches to cultivate and to tend with care and diligence.

Dreamwork is powerful and has long been intimately connected to witchcraft and shamanic practices. In the dreamworld, you're given an opportunity to connect to and engage with the land and spirits. Dreamwork requires that you open yourself and invite the spirit to speak so that you may listen. It also requires skills in discernment to be able to decipher your own personal sacred dream language.

Sleep is something that we do each day. It is a sacred act during which our bodies are given the opportunity to enter a completely relaxed state. When we sleep, our bodies heal, regenerate, and repair. When we sleep, we escape the stresses of our waking lives. Something that is *other* exists when we enter this sleep state. When our consciousness begins to blur and joins with that point just before we drift off to slumber, we are given a unique space in which to connect with spirit and be informed.

When I lived in my forest yurt, in the morning hours after the nighttime mists had lifted, the forest lit up with glowing green neon lichens and mosses covered in dew that reflected millions of tiny irides-cent rainbows. It was here that I encountered some of my most potent dreaming. The shape of my yurt was like that of a cauldron; it incubated and held me in my dreamy landscapes. My days were centered around waking and sleeping, in sync with the rising and setting of the sun. This balanced out my circadian rhythm and invited in rhythmic dreamtime synced with the waxing and waning of the moon.

I made a bedside altar dedicated to dream support and hung fragrant herbs around my bed to encourage lucidity. I slept with plants and tucked tarot cards and stones under my pillow. I sipped teas to help me sleep well and bring about fantastic dreams. Upon waking in the dawn hours, I poured myself some coffee and, among the swirling steam motes and incense, I wrote down my dreams—some of the most revealing dreams I've ever experienced.

One spring, a friend invited me to find and harvest some western skunk cabbage root. I was very interested in these plants because of their associations with hibernating bears waking in the spring to eat their roots. We climbed into his van and we found a swampy creek bed with hundreds of skunk cabbage flowers glowing like yellow lanterns. We set about digging up the massive root system of one plant, which took a great deal of effort. As I dug, the scent of rich earth, clean waters, and flowering skunk cabbage did something remarkable to my mind and heart. I knew that I needed to become more acquainted with the mysteries of these plants. And I knew that my dreams would be the best way to do it.

That night, I prayed and called upon the spirit of these plants, inviting them into my dreams. The following week, I experienced a direct connection with and understanding of them. They taught me how to utilize their medicine and showed me a path through the night, illuminated by their lanternlike inflorescences that lit the way to deeper dreamtime understanding.

Dreaming has the ability to shape your daily thoughts and actions. It gives you an access point from which you can connect to and commune with spirit. And it prepares you to take those messages into your waking life. How many times have strange, beautiful, and powerful images, thoughts, and ideas flashed through your mind during the moments just before you fall asleep? What is the earliest dream that you can recall? Have you ever had a dream carry over into your day, instilling fear, anxiety, hope, joy, laughter, or pleasure?

Some people are gifted at dreaming, while others feel they don't dream at all or can't recall what transpired in their dreams. We each possess the ability to dream. Moreover, we can awaken and cultivate this ability. Dreamwork, like many practices, takes *practice.* It takes time and effort to become proficient and adept at listening to your own sacred dream language. It takes patience and persistence.

Our modern culture works to disregard the potency of dreams and frowns upon daydreaming as well. As a child in elementary school, I was often scolded to stop daydreaming and get back to my math equations or writing tasks. But this only served to make me a better worker, not a better dreamer or a creator of magic and connection. It deadened my natural connection to spirit and divorced me further from my connection to the natural world.

Dreams are often disregarded as fluff, simply because dreaming does not benefit our capitalist culture, which is centered around productivity. Our society prefers rational thought to seemingly irrational dreams, because dreaming and daydreaming defy conformity. If you find yourself prone to daydreaming, protect this precious gift and learn how to flow with it to connect more deeply with spirit. This is your invitation to begin cultivating good dreaming practices and invite spirit to speak to you in the sacred language and images you innately understand.

## The Language of Dreams

Interpreting the language of dreams is a tricky game. I encourage you not to buy dream dictionaries and to avoid using tacky dream-interpretation websites. Your dream language is yours and yours alone—it belongs to no one else. Many dream-interpretation websites and books don't support the deeper meanings behind the symbols and occurrences you experience in your dream space. Over time, you can develop your own lexicon of dream symbols and their meanings.

What is a good dream to me may be a bad omen for another. Many years ago, I worked with a deity to whom snakes were sacred. During my time with this deity, I encountered venomous snakes in my dreams and was very frequently bitten by them. For me, this was a good sign, as it represented encountering my own fears and being able to alchemize the venom into wisdom and understanding. But my mother, who is deathly afraid of snakes, interpreted these dreams as bad omens and nightmares. It's wise to take into consideration the context and historical connection that you have with any dreamtime symbols and experiences you encounter. They are uniquely your own and, with time, will evolve in meaning in ways that dream dictionaries cannot provide.

Dreams in which I died have also become sacred to me and, over time, have taught me to face my fear of death and surrender to it. Death in dreams often signifies a deep and radical transformation. Very often, it is linked to processes of initiation. So if you do experience death dreams, know that you're being reshaped and reborn. Sometimes spirits do their work with us through the dream state, and this can include both death and initiation processes.

Although I warned above against using dream-interpretation websites and books, one of the best ways to learn to interpret your dreams is to do research on the items, themes, and experiences that appear in them. Avoid spiritually oriented websites, however, as counterintuitive as that may sound. Many of these websites can be appropriative of other cultures and filled with misinformation.

For example, say a bear shows up quite significantly in your dream. Research bear behaviors, what foods they eat, what their hibernation cycles are like, what their courtship rituals are when breeding, how they care for their young, and so forth. What role do bears play in your ecology? How do they interact with other species? How are they presented in folklore and myth? See if they have any significance in your ancestral traditions. Trust me, you'll find so much more information in this way than you will at some "spirit animal" website. This same principle applies to plants, historical figures, deities, and dream symbols as well. Taking this approach allows for more room in understanding and interpretation. It also opens a multitude of realms through which to explore your experience and dream symbols.

As you cultivate your dreams, consider recording them in a dream journal (p. 157). In a dream journal, you can craft a consistent personal dictionary and dedicated reference in which you can mark the frequency and reoccurrence of your specific dream themes. Themes that reoccur are the ones to which you should pay attention. An excellent resource for guidance around the symbols and figures we encounter in dreams is Juan Eduardo Cirlot's *Dictionary of Symbols*.

## Dreamwork

If you believe you're not good at dreaming, that is sure to come true. Trusting in yourself and in the process is key in dreamwork. It can be very helpful to fall asleep chanting a mantra affirming to yourself that you will remember and recall your dreams. I know that this sounds very simple, but if you intentionally dwell on something before you fall asleep, it will weave itself into your dream life. Going to sleep with the intention of having a lucid dream or a specific encounter increases your chances of that happening. It is just a matter of training your brain and reminding yourself of your abilities.

Write down affirmations of your capacity to dream and recite them daily. This can encourage a mindset that can change your beliefs around your dreaming ability. You can say these affirmations throughout the day or just before bed. Put sticky notes on your bathroom mirror or by your bedside to remind yourself. You can even set reminders on your phone to go off throughout the day to further support your new mindset and beliefs. Here are a few affirmations you can use daily to shift your mind into a state that cultivates dreams:

"I dream with clarity."

"I remember and can recall my dreams."

"Spirit speaks to me through dreams, and I listen."

Your dreamtime may also be cyclical in nature. We don't always have a direct line to spirit. Sometimes our spirits listen; sometimes they don't. If you're a person who menstruates, you may notice your dream activity peaking around your menstrual cycle. If you follow the moon's cycles, you may find that your dreams really begin to take shape when the moon is dark. Take note of these cycles to see if you can find a pattern. When you do, support these peak times by being more present to them.

## Dream Spaces

In our modern world, the art of dreaming has been devalued. We're taught to rush through our days focused on maximum productivity. For many of us, this can mean rushing through the evening and crashing into bed with little or no thought given to creating space to wind down and slowly, more consciously, approach our sleep time. We need to make space for our dreams. And making this space isn't just a radical act of self-care; it directly defies our culture's desire to stamp out the sacred connection to dreaming and the divine.

To combat this, I invite you to cultivate space for quiet pre-bedtime rituals that do not involve smartphones, TVs, or laptops. Set aside some time and consider putting screens away at least an hour before you go to bed. Try it for one week as an experiment and take notes on how this affects your sleep cycle. You may just be surprised at the benefits.

This self-care hour before bedtime is a prime opportunity to take part in rituals that support sleep and dreamtime. Consider reading a book, drinking a relaxing tea, meditating, reflecting quietly, praying, or journaling. All these actions help you wind down and generate reminders of the sacred dream space you're about to enter.

Since sleep is critical for both physical and mental health, dreams tend to flow more easily when we are rested. Limiting your use of electronics one hour before bedtime can greatly benefit your ability to get good, restful sleep. Lumens and the "deadly blue light" from electronic devices and screens keep the brain in an awakened state and restrain the production of the hormone melatonin, which controls sleeping and waking cycles, also known as the circadian rhythm.

When you scroll on your phone, you also receive stimuli that can leave your mind quite distracted or disturbed. These inputs can really affect your dreams. If you do not create the space and conditions in which the spirits of dreaming can appear, they'll have a harder time coming through. I invite you to consider your dreamtime as an elusive creature with whom you're desperate to commune. If you create the mental space, set the environment, and show up for it, eventually the spirit will meet you there. As you learn what works for you, powerful and clear dreaming will come to you more easily, and you can begin to understand your gifts and abilities in this realm.

Cultivating actual space to encourage dreaming is important as well. Your bedroom should be a sanctuary, a den, an incubator in which your body can rest. Reimagine this space as most sacred, if you don't already see it that way.

For instance, the color of your bedsheets, pillows, and altar cloths can invite in certain energies:

- Red draws in passion, sexuality, and power.
- Pink encourages sweetness, calm, nurturing, and healing, especially connected to the heart.

- Blue stimulates calm, protection, and connection to watery elements (a wonderful color to support dreaming).

- White facilitates connection to spirit and your ancestors.

- Green establishes connection to plants, generative energies, and money.

- Brown signifies earth, stability, and grounding.

If you are able, I strongly recommend creating a space to devote to your dreams. This doesn't need to be elaborate, expensive, or big. A small, simple altar will suffice. Any bedside table can serve as a small dreamtime altar and makes a wonderful space where you can check in before bed. My altar is an upside-down wooden crate with a blue cloth on top.

What you choose to add to your dream altar is entirely up to you. This is an opportunity to express and exercise your creativity. Place a small bowl of water there to act as a conduit for dreams and to help filter nightmares. Add statues or figures of spirit allies with whom you wish to connect. Found objects like stones, feathers, and bones can work as well. Plant allies, as in my skunk cabbage story, are also powerful supporters of dreamtime.

Around the bedside, you can hang small charms, herbs, sachets, or art to adorn your space, especially around the headboard or wall near where your head rests. If you're prone to nightmares, these adornments can add protection and function as a calming boundary around your space.

## Dream Journals

If you don't write down your dreams, they may slip away from you forever. A dream journal provides you with a useful reference tool, but also with proof of your spirit contacts. Over time, this practice can dispel any doubts that creep into your mind that your dreams are superfluous phantoms. A dream journal also creates a record for your reflection. Sometimes you may have a dream that takes time to process. Personally, I have had some dreams that have taken years to understand. Being able to look back in your journal and remember the details of your dreams is highly important. If you take away one thing from this chapter, please let it be that you begin a dream journal. You won't regret it.

Although I suggested not using your smartphone around bedtime, it can be a helpful device for recording dreams when you wake in the middle of the night. Sometimes, you may experience a strong dream and wake up with it still fresh in your mind. This is the time to press your smartphone's record button and journal your dream digitally so that you can listen later when you're writing in your dream journal.

I know that journaling doesn't always work for everyone. If this really isn't your style, keeping a collection of recorded dreams on your smartphone can be helpful in documenting them. Or you can even type them up on a laptop to retain them for later reference. The bottom line is, you must record those dreams, as they can lead you down a starlit path of deeper understanding.

Pen-and-paper journaling may not work for everyone, however. If that is true for you, just choose a format that calls out to you and get into the journaling habit. Here are a few options from which you can choose:

> **Voice recording:** Record your thoughts digitally. This can be especially helpful when you wake up at 3:00 AM with an important dream and the very thought of grabbing a pen and paper and turning on a light seems hellish! You can take this a step further by using an app that transcribes your voice recordings into words so you can read and review them later.
>
> **Digital writing platforms:** Journal directly onto a digital notebook, then save it to your

computer for later review. When I wrote this book, I moved my journal writing to a program on my laptop to learn how to type faster. There are lots of options out there. Just find one that works for you and get started.

**Paper:** Try using different colored pens to show how you are feeling, or to indicate days of the week or specific themes or energies that appear in your dreams—for instance, green for prosperity or red for power. You can also use color to designate a particular time and space through which you're moving. Or use colored tabs to mark very important dreams or realizations.

Remember, your dream journal is for you alone and should reflect your own practice. Use what you like and what you have available to make your journaling as accessible and doable as possible. It doesn't matter *how* you do. Just do it!

Here's a simple journal structure you can use to get started:

- Date, lunar phase, any astrological notations, or even where you are in your menstrual cycle.

- Musings on where you are emotionally in your waking life, how you're feeling in your body, or what is going on in your environment.

- Any interactions with the spirit or deities with whom you are working.

- Any goals or dreams you wish to achieve.

And finally, add all the details you can remember about the objects, people, spirits, themes, and settings that appear in your dreams. The goal of a dream journal is to integrate all your waking experiences with those you encounter in your dreams and to help you interpret those experiences in ways that can inform your daily life and your practice. Remember: It's all connected.

## Spirit Allies

Dreaming with the spirits of the land is a bold act that takes careful consideration. In some cultures, sleeping under certain tree species can connect you with the fae, or the little people. Some say that you will be snatched away to the Otherworld, never to return. And before you engage in land and spirit-of-place dreamwork, be sure that you've read the discussion of wards and protection in chapter 4. For this sort of work, you'll want to set some guards in place, as you never know who or what you'll encounter.

Start with a tree in a local park or, if you have access to a yard, perhaps you can nap under that lilac bush of which you're so fond. Trees and plants that are historically known to be connected to dreamwork include hawthorn, hazel, elder, oak, blackthorn, ash, alder, juniper, and birch. You can dream with any tree or shrub, however. Remember, you can also bring any (safe) tree or plant into your bed to support your dreamwork. One of my favorite shrubs with which to dream is elder. In the summer, I collect elder twigs and sleep with them under my pillow.

Dreaming with the spirits of the land is quite simple and uncomplicated. Just take a nap in the location to which you wish to connect. This may be a meadow, a local park, or a stream. Running water is especially effective when you enter the dream state just before falling into sleep. Listen closely and you will hear the water singing or speaking to you. Another method is to collect dirt from an area to which you want to connect. Be sure to ask for the permission of the spirits who reside there before you go gathering, however, and be sure to leave an altar offering in its place. Place the dirt on your dream altar to act as a conduit. Notice any images that come to mind or feelings that arise and record them in your dream journal.

## Plant Allies

Plant allies can help facilitate dreaming in quite potent ways. Plants often act as gatekeepers and initiators in the dream space. When working with plants, I find that prayer and breathwork encourage them to help me with a desired outcome. Below, I give examples of herbs that I often work with during dreamtime, but you can literally work with any plants to get to know them better through your dreams.

Mugwort is a classic herb for dreamtime and a powerful one! This herb is connected to the moon and to the element of Water, both of which support dream activity and facilitate a deeper connection to the land and plants. Sleeping with a small pillow filled with mugwort or the fresh herb near your head acts as a conduit for powerful experiences, as it gives an animating and driving force to your dreams. My personal experiences with mugwort have ranged from feeling as if I were levitating in bed to helping unlock reoccurring dream patterns and gaining an even deeper understanding of other plants. If you're using it in tea, I advise that you start with very small doses. Mugwort doesn't so much encourage rest, as heighten the ability to be lucid and wakeful during dreamtime. Experiment carefully with this one. If you are nursing, pregnant, or plan to become pregnant, do not use mugwort.

Rosemary is a powerful protector of all spaces, especially when burned. A few sprigs around the bed can help protect and keep the space clear from unwanted spirits and energies. You can make a smoke bundle by tying sprigs of rosemary together and allowing them to dry before burning. Or you can create a loose incense with rosemary. Burn it on a charcoal disk or in a brazier in your bedroom to promote dreams and offer up protection. Rosemary is also used for remembrance, as it can be helpful in dream recall and when burned in the morning hours as you record and journal about your dreams.

The alluring and intoxicating scent of jasmine has been linked to heightening psychic abilities, creativity, and dreams. A light perfume oil or hydrosol of jasmine can be a helpful aid. Dab jasmine oil around your chest, neck, and head, or spritz the hydrosol on and around your pillows to promote dreaming.

The beautifully shaped pods of star anise are used in psychic work, as well as to encourage strong dream activity. Anise seed can be used as well. Anise helps promote pleasant dreaming and sends protection to your spirit. This herb also offers protection from nightmares when placed in a sachet and tucked under your pillow. Like rosemary, it can be burned as a loose incense.

Dandelion roots are not often thought of for their magical uses, but they are used in folk magic traditions to increase dreaming and clarity when doing divination. With their moon-like seed heads and deep tap roots, dandelions can connect you to both the earth and the heavens. Roasted dandelion root has a slight vanilla-caramel favor and can be blended with other herbs to make a fantastic dream tea. Use dandelion when you wish to enhance your psychic abilities and to dream well.

Frankincense is a most excellent resin to burn to "raise vibrations." This plant intensifies any magical work and aids in sanctifying a space. It also helps to clear an area of any negativity and to increase focus and concentration. Burning a little before bed can help to promote good dreaming activity and rest. Frankincense is also a beautiful perfume oil. Combine it with a little jasmine and apply it to your pulse points and temples, and you have a powerful and uplifting dream oil for sleep.

Marshmallow root, or althea, is used to attract good spirits. Place this on your altar in a small bowl or in a pouch to help connect to spirits with whom you wish to work. Be mindful of drinking this as a tea, however. Because it has a slightly mucilaginous texture to it, marshmallow can help you to "slip" between worlds.

Chamomile, which is often overlooked as an herb for dreaming, can calm nerves and act as an after-meal digestive. This herb protects against nightmares and can be inhaled to calm and sweeten your state of mind. Combined with dandelion root, chamomile makes a wonderful, gentle tea that can help you wind down in the evenings before bedtime. Use this herb in your tea blends or in a bowl or sachet placed by your head as you sleep.

Skullcap, while not necessarily for dreaming, can help with nervous anxiety and to calm the nerves after a long, stressful day. Skullcap helps with those anxious thought loops in which you may often find yourself stuck. These can lead to restless nights and insomnia. Use this herb in a tea or tincture blend to bring about restful sleep, calm the mind, wind down, and relax.

Passion flower, as herbalist Michael Moore says, "is a simple, uncomplicated sedative." If you find yourself prone to anxiety, restlessness, or insomnia, this herb may be helpful in lowering stress and sedating your mind in a gentle, non-intrusive way. If you find yourself restless, nervous, and agitated, blending this herb with some skullcap and chamomile makes a fantastic tea that promotes restful sleep.

Mint is often overlooked as a plant for dreamwork, but any mint variety can be used in teas and incense blends to encourage dreams. In fact, mint blends well with skullcap to provide a gentle, calming bedtime tea. I have found great success with the wild variety of mint known as nettle leaf, horsemint, and/or catnip, which grows wild in my region. When used in tea, this can bring about powerful dreams and stimulate creativity.

Lavender is a classic calming and aromatic flower that is not often considered for use in dream-tea blends. Give it a try, however, because it tastes great. But be sparing about your use, as too much can make a bitter tea. When burned, lavender lets off a sweet scent that calms the nerves and brings lightness to a space. Utilize this herb when you need calm before bed and to soothe the nerves. A small sachet near your pillow can help with sleep and is especially effective when combined with rosemary and mugwort.

Below are some tea-blend suggestions to drink around bedtime. Use a teaspoon of each herb in a ball strainer or an in-the-mug basket strainer. Steep the herbs in sixteen to eighteen ounces of freshly boiled water. As you add the herbs to your tea, pray over them individually and call them into their purpose. Please be mindful that if you are pregnant, plan to become pregnant, or are nursing, you should avoid mugwort.

Calming herbs include:

- Skullcap
- Passion flower
- Lavender
- Chamomile

Deep-dreaming herbs include:

- Dandelion root
- Mugwort
- Chamomile
- Marshmallow root
- Star anise, or anise (optional, as this flavor isn't agreeable to everyone)

Nightmare-protection herbs include:

- Chamomile
- Passion flower

- Peppermint

- Lavender

Flower essences can also serve as gentle vibrational allies that help create deep shifts within the mind and body. Here are just a few of the flowers associated with dreamwork:

- Angelica

- Black-eyed Susan

- Chaparral

- Clematis

- Evening primrose

- Forget-me-not

- Hornbeam

- Lavender

- Milkweed

- Morning glory

- Mugwort

- Rosemary

- Saint John's wort

- Star tulip

- White chestnut

When working with any of these plant allies, approach them with an open heart as you pray for their assistance and they will guide you, opening up your dream space, teaching you the mysteries of their own knowledge, and giving you insights into their medicinal uses.

### Practice: Entering the Dreamworld

This simple practice will help you pull together all the elements of dreamwork discussed above and use them to help you enter your own dreamworld. It can also help you to dream with intention.

Before you begin, set up a bedside table or your dream altar. On this space, place the following items:

- A small piece of paper and pen

- A glass of water

- Florida water, an alcohol-based perfume or cologne water often employed in spiritual work, or any dream-related herbs (optional)

- Incense to burn or tea to drink

Before bed, pour a glass of water into a clear glass container. This container doesn't need to be fancy; you can use a mason jar or your favorite cup. A clear vessel works best to promote clarity, although colors also work—especially blue, as it helps support dreams and lends some protection.

On the piece of paper, write down what you wish to dream about. For example, you may write: "May the mysteries of mugwort be revealed to me." Write this wish in an open-ended way or ask a question so that the spirit is prompted to reply. Then place the paper under the glass container of water. Whisper your question or petition over the water's surface. You can also burn some incense or sprinkle any herbs you prefer into the water. Add a few drops of Florida water to the container if you like. Meditate or pray, then allow yourself to drift into sleep, knowing that your question will be answered.

Even if you do not specifically dream of the situation in question, be sure to take note of what you dream about and record it in your dream journal. Allow whatever dreams you have to marinate, knowing that understanding will come with time. Repeat this practice as often as you need until you have your answer, or until something is revealed to you.

Lunar cycles are great to work with here, because the dark or new moon opens the door to spirit, and the full moon shines light and reveals the situation. And this is what dreamwork is all about. Remember: Your aim is wakefulness, and your enemy is dreamless sleep.

### Practice: Removing Roadblocks

You may encounter many internal roadblocks or fears taking up space as you develop your dreamwork practice. Make note of these occurrences. If these blockages are too strong, you may need to pause to reflect upon them before beginning. Write down what you feel is holding you back and bring the causes to the surface. A simple and helpful little spell is to write down these roadblocks and then burn the paper, thus ridding yourself of what is blocking you. Dispose of the ashes by placing them at a crossroad or simply dropping them in a trash can. There is absolutely nothing wrong with tossing your paper ashes in the trash. Just be sure that the flames are completely extinguished before doing so. Many witches get hung up on how to dispose of the remains of a spell, even one as simple as this. The trash works just fine, as it's where your blockages belong anyway.

## Chapter 8

# Committing to the Path

*Nature is made of cycles and we are made of nature.*
—V. E. Schwab

As we come to the end of this book, my hope is that you can see how the earth and witchcraft are inextricably entwined. Committing to one is committing to the other, and this commitment affirms that you are willing to embark on the journey toward spirit. This commitment can happen naturally in life many times over. You can be your own catalyst for it when you're ready to leap into the unknown or tread that dimly lit trail through the forest.

My own commitment rite was performed in the quiet evening hours, before my gods, the spirits, and the land. I put a ring on my finger at the finish of it to signify a marriage to my higher self, as it were. It's been a constant physical reminder of who I am and what I want, and of my ties to the land and to spirit—a constant reminder that I am a *witch*. I don't ever want to forget that. I wear that ring, with its small moon-stone set in silver, to this day. It's tarnished and worn down from hours of digging in dirt, touching rocks, and generally living life. It's chipped and scratched and well-worn. Yet it still shines bright, reminding me of my purpose.

A self-initiation rite like this can usher in both dramatic and subtle changes. It really depends on where you are and what your circumstances are. Follow your intuition. Listen to your heart. Let it guide you.

You may, at some point, wish to commit yourself to the witches' path through a self-initiatory rite that symbolically sets you firmly on the path to spirit. This kind of rite can commit you to the next phase of your journey. It also sends out a ripple into the universe and to spirit that you're ready to show up and walk the path placed before you. Performing a commitment rite can also generate a shift within you and give you a place from which to start your new journey. Or it can validate the path you're already walking.

The rite of self-initiation I give below is the same one I performed ten years ago—the rite that forever set me upon this path I walk. When I performed this rite, it enabled me to accept and embody the title of witch fully. It opened the door to spirit for me. The crooked and wandering path that witches tread—the journey to which we commit and by which we are bewitched—is terrifyingly beautiful to behold. It is not a straight and narrow path, however. In fact, it's just the opposite. And sometimes it disappears altogether in the darkness and we are forced to wander by starlight.

Walking the crooked and winding path of the witch requires a life-time commitment to plumbing the spiritual depths of the world around us. And it can be difficult to maintain this commitment in the individualistic society in which we live. The truth is, it is impossible to live a life free from capitalism, because we are so deeply entrenched in it. The only possible end to our path is death. And even in that, there is the beginning of something new as we merge with the stars and the spiritual life around us.

Before I set foot on this path, I knew that the calling I felt within me was something I could not ignore or deny. I knew that if I went to my death bed without exploring this strange pathway lit by stars and the glowing night embers, I would die miserable, longing for something that I'd never explored. So I took a deep breath and cast myself into the depths, uncovering what was hidden, lost, and secret within me and around me. I do not regret the past, nor do I wish to shut the door on it. But I found the one door—the one that was slightly ajar, through which I could glimpse spirit—and I took a step through it. I invite you to do the same.

Witches reject the status quo. We live lives free from the oppression of acceptable cultural standards and social mores. The lifestyle of a practicing witch opens us up entirely, allowing us to embrace the lessons of the past and future and to live authentic lives without damaging those who live around us. And this includes *all* earthly forms. We listen to the land and its inhabitants. We remember our origins and we honor the environment we inhabit. We invite in our ancestors and our non-human kin to help guide us on our journey. We listen. We orient ourselves. And we find presence and belonging in the spirit of the place where we stand.

I encourage you to go forth, strangely, into that night.

### Practice: Self-Initiation Rite

For this rite of commitment and dedication you will need:

- A ring or necklace that you can wear comfortably for the rest of your life

- A four-inch candle in white or light blue

- A glass of water

- Blessing oil, plain olive oil, or any oil oriented to your purpose

- A small heat-proof cup or glass bowl with a flat bottom

- Any representations of the spirits and/or gods with whom you work

- A written dedication or prayer from the heart

First, choose a moon phase or an important date on which to perform your rite, then build a small altar. This can be built on your working altar, or you can create a whole new space from which to work. Place representations of your spirits and/or gods around the altar and put a glass of water on it.

Carve your name into the candle along with your intention, then dress the candle with the oil and set it to the side. Hold the ring or necklace in your dominant hand and charge it with energy from your free hand. Place it on your altar and place the cup or bowl upside-down over it. Burn the bottom of the candle and let a little wax drip onto the bottom of the cup or bowl, then stick the candle on top of the dripped wax. This will hold it in place.

Let the wax cool to ensure that the candle is held securely, then light the candle and recite your written prayer or pray from the heart your intention of dedication. Speak to your ancestors, gods, and spirits, telling them why you're here and what you intend to do. Ask for their support and guidance. Allow the candle to burn down completely. If you perform this rite at night or in the evening, you can let the candle burn while you sleep. This can encourage the incubation of dreams that may portend any omens or signs.

Upon awakening, you are born anew. Wear the ring or necklace as an act of dedication and a forever reminder that you're walking the path of the witch.

# Conclusion

This book was born out of my online course called Praxis of the Witch, which I launched in 2019. The course was designed to help others integrate witchcraft practices into their daily lives. And this commitment became the bones of this book. Many people have taken this course over the years, and the feedback I have received from them indicates that it did, indeed, provide a framework in which others could expand their practice.

To be honest, I didn't want to write a book. I've never really considered myself a writer. But spirit thrust this project into my lap and I couldn't say no. Honestly, what I wanted to do was pack up my truck and run for the desert—into dreamy hot days spent with plants, rocks, coyote yips, and dirt clinging to my legs. I wanted to squint into an endless bright horizon of sagebrush steppe. Instead, I prayed on the matter and was given a clear answer: This is my work. So I set to the task.

A unique set of circumstances arose at the beginning of this book project. First, I got sober. Second, I rediscovered the God of my understanding. And third, with time and prayer, I came to realize that this book was a devotional work to Our Lady, the Holy Mother, Inanna, Mary—whatever name you prefer. You don't have to believe in anything to read this book, but you must understand that the Holy Mother's presence and guiding hand are laced within these pages. Without her, this book would not have been possible.

Both the course and the book unfolded at a time when so many of us were forced into our internal landscapes and made to face a looming threat. Many who took my course hoped to find some solace in it. They realized that, even in this age of disconnection, the land has always been calling to them. They just needed an opportunity to show up, to really listen, and to take part. They were called back to a recognition of the spirits of the land as an escape from the constant drone of the news cycle and the isolation inherent in social media and online distractions. More and more, people are feeling the need to venture forth into the land and to see it in a different light—as a place of comfort where they can forge a deeper connection to the life that flows around them. This book seeks to deepen that connection and take it a step further. For we are not just living on the land, we are living *with* it. My wish is that the culture at large comprehend the magnitude of this connection.

Writing this book was a spiritual experience. I suffered from a debilitating bout of imposter syndrome as I began, but I found through the grace of my spiritual practice that this book wasn't about me or even for me. This book is for you, dear reader. This book is for the Holy Mother, who sustains all life on this blessed planet. This book is for the land—for the many lands— that have held and supported me. Once I put the writing of this book into the hands of a power greater than myself, it magically took shape (with the help of my lovely editors). Without the Holy Mother, without the land, this book would not have been possible.

It is my hope, dream, and desire that this book ushers you forth into a new practice, or that it affirms and validates the path you are on. Witchcraft is impossible to define and, as such, it is unique to each of us. It will manifest differently in each of our lives; it will take a different trajectory for each of us. Please remember that your craft does not need to look like the craft of others. Your craft is your own. The primary commonality across the practice of being a witch is that it is rooted in the earth—in the land we inhabit and all that it contains. From there, we each find our own orientation; we each proceed in our own practice.

I am not good at endings, so let this book be the beginning of something new and beautiful for you. Be weird, be wild, and remember—do witchcraft.

# Appendix A: List of Practices

**Chapter 7**

**Chapter 8**

# Acknowledgments

I would like to thank Bud at Hierophant Publishing for seeing something I could not. To Kirsten, who listened to me day after day hashing out the intricacies of this book, and for giving me valuable feedback. You're a dear friend and companion witch on this path. To Peter Michael Bauer for answering all my questions and for writing excellent books on rewilding that have greatly impacted my practice. For my twelve-step recovery community, always supporting me and keeping me sober. To my partner, Steve, for holding my hand and loving me when I was down on myself. To J. Allen Cross, fellow witch and author, who also held my hand in moments of pure doubt. And to the countless others who have supported me in the creation of this book and given me unconditional love—I thank you all.

# Suggested Readings

Anderson, Cora. *Fifty Years in the Feri Tradition.*

Anonymous. *The Black Pullet.*

Cochrane, Robert. *The Robert Cochrane Letters: An Insight into Modern Traditional Witchcraft.*

Coleman, Martin. *Communing with the Spirits: The Magical Practice of Necromancy.*

Cowan, Elliot. *Plant Spirit Medicine: A Journey into the Healing Wisdom of Plants.*

Cunningham, Scott. *Cunningham's Encyclopedia of Magical Herbs.*

de Mattos Frisvold, Nicholaj. *Craft of the Untamed: An Inspired Vision of Traditional Witchcraft.*

——————. *Pomba Gira and the Quimbanda of Mbùmba Nzila.*

Dimech, Alkistis and Peter Grey. *The Brazen Vessel.*

Estés, Clarissa Pinkola. *Women Who Run with the Wolves.*

Evans-Wentz. *The Fairy-Faith in Celtic Countries.*

Frazer, James George. *The Golden Bough.*

Green, James. *Herbal Medicine-Maker's Handbook: A Home Manual.*

Grey, Peter. *Apocalyptic Witchcraft.*

——————. *The Red Goddess.*

Grimassi, Raven. *Communing with the Ancestors: Your Spirit Guides, Bloodline Allies, and the Cycle of Reincarnation.*

Heaven, Ross and Howard G. Charing. *Plant Spirit Shamanism: Traditional Techniques for Healing the Soul.*

Heliophilus. *The Green Book.*

Huson, Paul. *Mastering Witchcraft: A Practical Guide for Witches, Warlocks, and Covens.*

Leland, Charles G. *Aradia or the Gospel of the Witches.*

Mickaharic, Draja. *A Century of Spells.*

——————. *Spiritual Cleansing: A Handbook of Psychic Protection.*

Miller, Jason. *Protection and Reversal Magick.*

——————. *The Sorceror's Secrets: Strategies in Practical Magick.*

Miller, Richard Alan. *Magical and Ritual Use of Aphrodisiacs.*

——————. *Magical and Ritual Use of Herbs.*

Moore, Michael. *Medicinal Herbs of the Mountains West.*

Müller-Ebeling, Claudia, Christian Rätsch, and Wolf-Dieter Storl. *Witchcraft Medicine: Healing Arts, Shamanic Practices, and Forbidden Plants.*

Nichols, Mike. *The Witches Sabbats.*

Pearson, Nigel G. *Treading the Mill: Practical Craft Working in Modern Traditional Witchcraft.*

Pendell, Dale. *The Pharmako Trilogy.*

Redgrove, Peter and Penelope Shuttle. *The Wise Wound.*

Scout, Urban. *Rewild or Die.*

Simard, Suzanne. *Discovering the Wisdom of the Forest.*

Starhawk. *The Spiral Dance.*

Valiente, Doreen. *Natural Magic.*

——————. *Rebirth of Witchcraft.*

——————. *Witchcraft for Tomorrow.*

Vaudoise, Mallorie. *Honoring Your Ancestors: A Guide to Ancestral Veneration.*

Wilby, Emma. *Cunning-Folk and Familiar Spirits: Shamanistic Visionary Traditions in Early Modern British Witchcraft and Magic.*

——————. *The Visions of Isobel Gowdie: Magic, Witchcraft, and Dark Shamanism in Seventeenth-Century Scotland.*

Wood, Matthew. *The Book of Herbal Wisdom: Using Plants as Medicines.*

Worth, Valerie. *Crone's Book of Charms and Spells.*

. . . . . . . . . . . . . . . . . . . . . . . . . . . . . . . . . . . . . . . . . . . . . . . . .

Hier○phant publishing

books that inspire your body, mind, and spirit

San Antonio, TX

www.hierophantpublishing.com